THE
FOUR SEASONS

OF SHAKER LIFE

An Intimate Portrait
of the Community
at Sabbathday Lake

_____

GERARD C. WERTKIN

Photographs by
ANN CHWATSKY

A FIRESIDE BOOK
Published by Simon & Schuster, Inc.
New York

IN MEMORY OF BROTHER THEODORE E. JOHNSON (1931-1986)

A FIRESIDE BOOK
PUBLISHED BY SIMON & SCHUSTER, INC.
SIMON & SCHUSTER BUILDING
ROCKEFELLER CENTER
1230 AVENUE OF THE AMERICAS
NEW YORK, NEW YORK 10020
FIRESIDE AND COLOPHON ARE REGISTERED
TRADEMARKS OF SIMON & SCHUSTER, INC.
DESIGNED BY EVE METZ
MANUFACTURED IN THE UNITED STATES OF
AMERICA

10   9   8   7   6   5   4   3   2

LIBRARY OF CONGRESS CATALOGING IN
PUBLICATION DATA
WERTKIN, GERARD C.
    THE FOUR SEASONS OF SHAKER LIFE.

    "A FIRESIDE BOOK."
    BIBLIOGRAPHY: P.
    INCLUDES INDEX.
    1. SABBATHDAY LAKE (ME.) 2. POLAND SPRING
(ME.)—CHURCH HISTORY, I. TITLE.
BX9768.S2W47 1986   289'.8   86-4650
ISBN: 0-671-61815-6

CONTENTS

Author's Preface

MY JOURNEY ALONG THE PLEASANT PATHS and byways of Shaker Village began one summer afternoon in 1966 in an appropriately simple manner, without any hint of what I would find. Intrigued by a newspaper article about the Maine community, I wrote to one of the Shaker sisters seeking more information about the museum at Sabbathday Lake and the availability of publications on the Society's history and current situation. I knew almost nothing of these people, but was struck by the improbability of their survival in the twentieth century and curious about the continuity of their religious traditions and way of life. It was highly uncharacteristic for me to have written that letter. Did I suspect then, almost twenty years ago, how many letters would follow, or how many visits?

My inquiry resulted in a warm and engaging invitation from Sister R. Mildred Barker, a trustee of the Society, to come and see for myself. This was the beginning of an absorbing exploration into many aspects of Shaker life and creativity. But although Shaker Village would become as familiar to me as my own home, it would never be just an ordinary place, another destination for a long summer weekend. After two decades of frequent visits to the Village and considerable study of its ways, I would continue to be moved by the historic witness of the Shakers, surprised by the wonderful diversity of their gifts and humble in the face of mysteries that would remain locked to my understanding.

My first attendance at Shaker meeting, which occurred a year or two after my introduction to the Believers and their lovely village, represented a turning point in this exploration. Having read of the Society's traditional distinction between public meetings and family worship, I had been hesitant to ask for the privilege of attending religious services, although I knew that others had been welcomed. When I finally did ask, the spontaneous warmth with which Sister Frances A. Carr responded to my request assured me that my presence would not be viewed by the family as an intrusion upon its privacy. But nothing that I had read prepared me for that memorable meeting, for there I found not the assembled remnant of some failed utopia, as many in the world suggested, but a community secure in its faith and alive to the transcendent possibilities it brought to their lives. In words and song, these Believers, each according to his or her own individual gifts, spoke simply, but often eloquently, not only of a shared past but of a present of many rich and varied textures, and of a future resonant with hope.

Shaker meeting is an intimate affair, even when it addresses cosmic concerns. Periods of awesome silence alternate with personal testimony as, one by one, the worshippers respond to the moving of the spirit among them. I sat that quiet Sunday morning in the family chapel of the great brick dwellinghouse, feeling that I had been admitted into a private world, where generations of Believers had transmitted and maintained a sacred heritage unknown to the world at large. On the sisters' side of the room, the eldress and two trustees of the church, each wearing the distinctive Shaker cap, sat facing the little congregation. My place was with Brother Theodore E. Johnson on the brethren's side, two men among ten women, but somehow the room did not appear empty. The Believers filled it with the strength of their presence.

It is a tradition at Sabbathday Lake to begin the service of worship with biblical readings, a homily and two "set songs," frequently chosen from one of the Society's several printed hymn books, before opening the meeting to individual testimony and spontaneous singing from the Believers' vast, oral repertory of religious folk music.

I remember the first hymn, or set song, that we sang together that long ago Sunday morning. It was from *Shaker Music: Original Inspirational Hymns and Songs Illustrative of the Resurrection Life and Testimony of the Shakers* (New York, 1884), a book that I held in my hand, not quite believing that a volume so old was still in active use. (I was later to learn that this was one of the "newer" collections of Shaker music.) The song was "Redeeming Love" by Eldress Mary Ann Gillespie (1829–1887) of the Maine ministry, a gifted leader whose memory continues to be cherished by the Sabbathday Lake Shakers almost one hundred years after her death. Sister Mildred often says that Eldress Mary Ann's songs speak directly to the heart. I know that I was touched by it that Sunday morning; it seemed to capture the very essence of the meeting.

As we sang this old song, I was able to see much of the south portion of the Village from the large window near me, the green lawns and shade trees, the Trustees' Office and the neat, back row of white buildings, and in the distance, the barns, pastures and meadows, quiet in the warmth of the summer morning. It may have been the still beauty of the setting, the strength and dignity of the singers, or something more profound, but the words of Eldress Mary Ann's refrain did not seem incongruous to me. If anywhere the heavens and earth could blend, I thought, it was here.

As the years passed, I often remembered this first meeting, for so much of the life and faith of the Shakers was opened to me then. I felt free to stand among the Believers and repeat the ancient Hebrew words of a prayer from my own religious heritage, knowing that they did not want me to be anything but myself, just as they were true to themselves. Years ago, Brother Ted observed that there were no masks among Believers. It is a Shaker principle that only in stripping away artifice and conceit can true freedom be realized. Simplicity, as mediated for us by the Shakers, is not some form of cold austerity, but a continuing process of self-discovery. I learned then that every facet of Shaker life may be seen as the product of a surprisingly progressive and affirmative system of belief.

The Shakers have always pointed to their religious tradition as the source of the innovative technology and genius for invention that has marked their history. The basic assumption of Shaker faith that life and all its processes are progressive, has encouraged a creative spirit among Believers, while the freedom from want provided by their communal environment has permitted experimentation. A social structure offering women equality with men in all departments of community life is but a practical application of the Shaker concept of Mother and Father in God. And, of course, the Shaker tradition in arts and crafts cannot be fully understood without reference to a spiritual approach that exalts simplicity, harmony and perfection not only as goals of the religious life, but as proofs of its efficacy.

At a critical time in the history of America's oldest continuing religious community, it appears especially appropriate that its traditions, ways of life and hopes for the future be documented. While there is a growing body of literature about the Shaker movement, no effort has been undertaken to record the life of a living Shaker community and its members, both in photographs and words, within the context of their history and faith. Telling their story is the purpose of this book.

Redeeming Love

ALFRED, ME.

1. The dark-ness of the night is pass'd, The morn-ing light is break - ing,
2. The wa - ters of re - deem-ing love Are flow - ing as a riv - er,
3. The veil of darkness now is rent, And migh- ty truths are roll - ing,

And saints a-bove, in songs of love To mu - sic now are wak - ing.
Deep fountains of the heart are stirred; Oh, praise the Lord for- ev - er!
As we approach the mer- cy- seat God's glo-ry is un - fold - ing.

Lift up your voic-es, kin-dred souls, The heav'ns and earth are blending;

I see the an - gels of the Lord In clouds of light de- scend - ing.

1. The darkness of the night is pass'd,
   The morning light is breaking,
   And saints above, in songs of love,
   To music now are waking.

   Lift up your voices, kindred souls,
   The heav'ns and earth are blending;
   I see the angels of the Lord
   In clouds of light descending.

2. The waters of redeeming love,
   Are flowing as a river,
   Deep fountains of the heart are stirred;
   Oh, praise the Lord forever!

3. The veil of darkness now is rent,
   And mighty truths are rolling,
   As we approach the mercy seat,
   God's glory is unfolding.

9

A Word About the Photographs

DURING THE AMERICAN FOOD FESTIVAL ON Shaker cooking at the Vista International Hotel in New York City, I first met Sister Frances A. Carr, the kitchen deaconess of the Sabbathday Lake Community. I was amazed and delighted to be talking with and photographing this lovely vibrant woman whom I had previously thought of as belonging to a past culture. I admired her competence, her friendliness and her kindness, and we became friends. Through her, I met Sister Mildred and Brother Ted and, again, I was struck by both their specialness and their realness.

When I visited them in Maine for the first time, on a clear fall day, I was awed by the beauty of the surroundings and overwhelmed by the philosophy that had led them to where they are now. I was privileged to stay with them and share their hospitality and their way of life. Through their gracious openness I soon learned much about their history, religion and crafts.

My passion as a photographer is to achieve a deep understanding of other people's lives. Other ways of living fascinate me and the Shakers drew me immediately. When I visit them in Maine I feel an inner sense of order and calm that comes in few other places. "Hands to work and hearts to God" is a creed so visible in the energetic community at Sabbathday Lake that I can feel very strongly the mystical presence of the Shaker legacy. I do not envision the end of the community but rather share their belief that the band of eight will prosper. I hope my camera has done them justice.

ANN CHWATSKY

Acknowledgments

The Four Seasons of Shaker Life could not have been written without the interest, patience and cooperation of the Sabbathday Lake Shakers. I am pleased to acknowledge with deep and abiding gratitude the kindness of Sisters Minnie Greene, Marie Burgess and the late Elizabeth Dunn who welcomed me and my family to their Village and opened their hearts to us. The late Sister Eleanor M. Philbrook, for many years senior trustee of the Society, was my frequent hostess at the Trustee's Office; her genial hospitality and commitment to service won her the respect and admiration of many in the world. Sister Elsie A. McCool, in correspondence or in conversation in her sewing room at the Sisters' Shop, has shared with me her considerable knowledge of the community, its history and lore; I am grateful to her for her many acts of kindness through the years. I have shared almost two decades of friendship with Sister Frances A. Carr; she deserves my appreciation not only for placing her special insights and understanding of Shaker ways at my disposal, but for allowing me to use her recipes in this book. My gratitude to her is too deeply felt to express adequately here.

During many visits to Shaker Village, Brother Wayne Smith has offered his assistance in a variety of helpful ways, and Brother Arnold Hadd has drawn from his vast knowledge of the details of community history in responding to my questions; I acknowledge my indebtedness to both of these young brethren. Brother Theodore E. Johnson's contributions to the field of Shaker studies are of inestimable importance. His meticulous scholarship has had a direct impact on this book; I have drawn from his important publications and from *The Shaker Quarterly*, which he edited for the Society from 1961 to 1974. My own understanding of the Shaker way in Maine has been illumined by Brother Theodore's deep insights into the traditions and faith of the Church. He has graciously shared information with me and allowed me to have access to the community's library and archives. For all these kindnesses, and many more, I am grateful to him.

From the first time I visited Sabbathday Lake, Sister R. Mildred Barker has been friend and guide. Thoroughly devoted to the community and schooled in its ways, she has provided leadership and inspiration during much of the long and fruitful life she has spent among Believers. Although full of the grace and wisdom of years, Sister Mildred retains the lively spirit of Shakerism; she brings to everything she does its simple and direct integrity. But for her encouragement to visit Shaker Village and to learn its traditions, I would not have walked the paths that led to the writing of this book. I am profoundly indebted to her.

Other friends and associates also offered helpful assistance and advice. I am grateful to Francisco F. Sierra for preparing the map and diagrams used in this book; Peter Ginsberg for useful suggestions and counsel; and Tom Robinson for typing the manuscript. I owe much to my friends at Simon & Schuster, especially to Barbara Gess for her creative collaboration and extraordinary editorial skills, and Eve Metz for the sensitivity of her design. And, of course, my thanks to Ann Chwatsky who through all four seasons of the Shaker year brought enthusiasm, commitment and inspiration to the project.

GERARD C. WERTKIN

For Barbara Gess, who had the vision. For Eve Metz, who had the sight. For Stacey Holston, who "covered" the book so well. For my family, who were able to share the experience with me. For Jessica, who began it all. For Mady, Sharon, Tom and Peter, who were there for me . . . thanks. A special acknowledgment to Anahid and Vincent of Diana Labs and, of course, thanks to the Shakers at Sabbathday Lake, Maine.

ANN CHWATSKY

Sitting, left to right: Sisters
Minnie Greene, R. Mildred
Barker, Marie Burgess,
Frances A. Carr. Standing,
left to right: Sister Elsie A.
McCool, Brothers Theo-
dore E. Johnson, Wayne
Smith, Arnold Hadd

A CHOSEN LIFE

FROM A VANTAGE POINT HIGH ON A GENTLY sloping hill, standing amid rows of apple trees, you can see much of the Shaker Village and, beyond it, the lake from which it takes its name. But for the presence of an imposing brick dwellinghouse, the cluster of white frame buildings and the red barn might be taken for any large, well-maintained family farm. Sheds for farm equipment and machinery stand adjacent to pastures for grazing sheep. Vegetable gardens, rows of cultivated herbs and fields planted in hay stretch out to the woodlands covering much of the Shaker Society's nineteen hundred acres.

But if Sabbathday Lake is not the remote and secluded settlement that many assume a Shaker village to be, it is anything but ordinary, for here a people set themselves apart in pursuit of a vision two hundred years ago. It is, for them, hallowed ground, a place of shared traditions and impressive accomplishment; of fidelity to a faith brought to America from England in 1774 and of consecration to a difficult and often misunderstood way of life. It is also a place of strange and wonderful occurrences. The Shakers call it Chosen Land.

If the apple orchard provides a vantage point from which to see the whole of Shaker Village, it is also a fitting place to begin this exploration of Shaker life at Sabbathday Lake. In one of the many stories preserved by Believers about the founder of their faith, Mother Ann Lee, the apple tree is presented as a metaphor for the Shaker experience.

Hannah Kendall was once with Mother, on her journey from Ashfield to Petersham [Massachusetts], and they came to an apple tree in full blossom. Mother looked at it and said, "How beautiful this tree is now! But some of the apples will soon fall off; some will hold on longer; some will hold on till they are full half grown, and then fall off; and some will get ripe.

"So it is with souls who set out in the way of God. Many will set out very fair, and soon fall away; some will go further, and then fall off; some will go further still, and then fall; and some will go through."

It is not surprising that the Shakers of Sabbathday Lake often repeat this story. They have

seen a steady, apparently unremitting disintegration of Shaker life elsewhere. Once, nineteen or twenty principal villages, with five thousand or more members, were to be found in New York, Massachusetts, Connecticut, New Hampshire, Maine, Ohio, Kentucky and Indiana, as well as a number of smaller centers in these and other states. One by one they have closed their doors, never to reopen. Only at Sabbathday Lake is the traditional Shaker way of life being led today in its fullness, although several sisters continue to reside at Canterbury, New Hampshire, now restored and operated as a museum by Shaker Village, Inc. As in the tale of the apple tree, the Believers of Maine have held on to their faith and they seem determined to "go through." They also have kept the door open for others who would follow in their path. This dedication, at a time when only eight of them respond to the call to meeting, is part of the wonder of their story.

Village and Lake

SABBATHDAY LAKE is situated in the northwestern corner of the town of New Gloucester in Cumberland County in south central Maine. The name carries an appropriate suggestion of New England piety about it; but, surprisingly, it may be traced back beyond the repose of a long succession of Village Sundays to an earlier time, when the region was still a wilderness and not even the sound of a church bell distinguished the Sabbath from the other days of the week. According to local lore, the name grew out of the custom of the first white explorers in the area to gather at lakeshore every Sunday in the early 1700s to visit with each other and share tales of their backwoods adventures. These hunters called the body of water the "Sabbath-day Pond", a name which soon came to designate the locality as well. More likely, it is a corruption of the word *sabaday* or *sabada*, which is said to mean "provision cache" or "thoroughfare" in the language of the Abnaki Indians who lived in stockaded settlements throughout much of Maine and New Brunswick.

Meetinghouse exterior. Separate entryways are used by brethren and sisters.

Museum exhibit. Pine and maple tailoring counter, Sabbathday Lake, ca. 1850

From the Shaker orchard

Today, summer cottages and camps dot the wooded shores of Sabbathday Lake, an expanse of water two miles long by one-half mile wide. At its northern end is an outlet to the Royal River (called "Royal's River" until this century) which wends its way through the Maine countryside until it reaches the Atlantic at Yarmouth, eighteen miles away. Only a rippling stream as it flows from the lake, the Royal River was the highway upon which the first settlers in this part of the country arrived on rafts in the years following the grant in 1736 of a township to sixty inhabitants of Gloucester, Massachusetts, by the General Court of the Province.

Although much of the western and northern shores of the lake lie on Shaker land, the village and lake did not share the same name for many years. The first properties to comprise Shaker Village when it was organized in the late eighteenth century were still within the southeastern limits of Thompson's Pond Plantation, then a narrow, unincorporated strip of land running almost nine miles northwesterly from the Village to Otisfield. Eventually, portions of Thompson's Pond Plantation were annexed to the several towns adjoining it, and Shaker Village became part of New Gloucester in 1816. Sometime later in the first half of the nineteenth century (no one seems to know exactly when), a post office designated West Gloucester was established in the Shaker community. But after fifty years, continuing confusion with West Gloucester, *Massachusetts*, led to a decision to adopt the old name for the vicinity. In 1890, Eldress Elizabeth Noyes, the Village postmistress, received a notice from the postal authorities advising her that the designation of the local office was to be changed to Sabbathday Lake. The name has clung to the Village and its immediate surroundings ever since, although the nation's last Shaker post office closed on June 30, 1955.

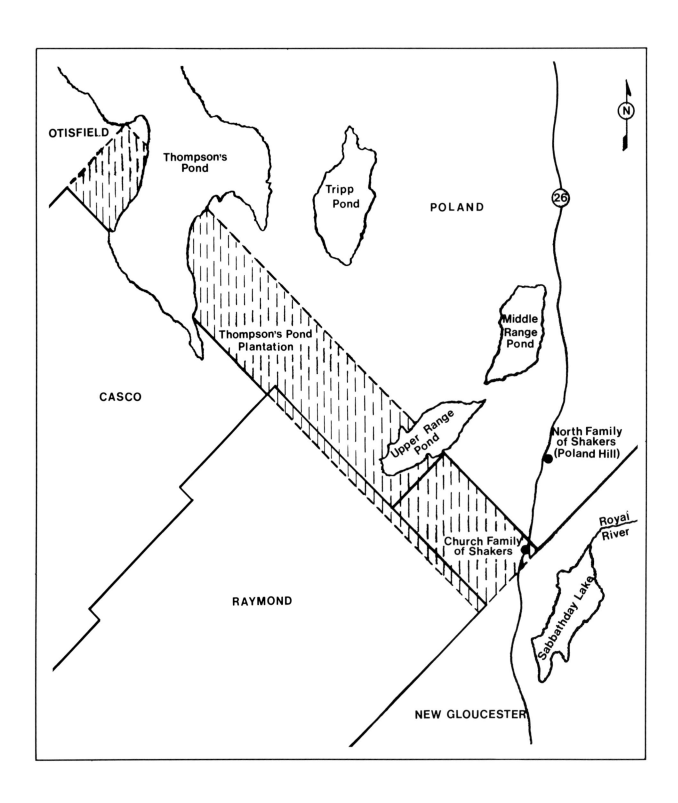

OTISFIELD

Thompson's
Pond

Tripp
Pond

POLAND

26

CASCO

Thompson's Pond
Plantation

Middle
Range
Pond

Upper Range
Pond

North Family
of Shakers
(Poland Hill)

Church Family
of Shakers

Royal
River

RAYMOND

Sabbathday Lake

NEW GLOUCESTER

N

Shaker Survival in Maine

SOME SAY THAT the difficulty of life in the harsh Maine countryside and the relative lack of wealth of the little Society prompted the survival of the Shaker way in Maine. The need to put "hands to work and hearts to God," to use the words of a famous Shaker maxim, left little time for considering alternatives. In addition, the rural location of the Maine community allowed the Believers to go about their daily rounds without coming into unwanted contact with the "world" until well into the twentieth century. If this resulted in some backwardness, it also reinforced the sort of Yankee determination and fortitude long associated with New England country folk. But these factors alone would not have ensured survival if it were not for an unbroken line of revered teachers and leaders who, even in this century, continued to excite in new generations the spiritual possibilities of a life dedicated wholly to God.

Among the great leaders of latter-day Shakerism at Sabbathday Lake was Sister Aurelia Mace (1835–1910), who served as teacher, trustee and associate eldress. Her bright and inquiring mind sought out the important thinkers of her time. She corresponded with Tolstoy and with poets and politicians, entertained visitors from many walks of life and wrote for the public press. Through her own example, she gathered a group of young sisters, her "ten gems of priceless worth," as she called them, who would continue traditions to which she had dedicated her life. Among these was Eldress Prudence Stickney, who led the Sabbathday Lake Shakers until her death in 1950 at the age of ninety. Concerned for the welfare of her people, Eldress Prudence encouraged the consolidation of Maine's other remaining Shaker community, at Alfred in York County, with the Sabbathday Lake Society in 1931. This joining of forces greatly enhanced the prospects of the faith in Maine.

Eldress Harriett Coolbroth (1862–1952), who herself had gathered many souls to the cause, came to Sabbathday Lake from Alfred in 1931. An inspired leader, Eldress Harriett was a staunch Believer who preserved hundreds of the old Shaker songs transmitted to her in a continuous tradition. Much of the fervor of the religious life of Sabbathday Lake today can be traced to her dedication. One of Eldress Harriett's "girls" was Sister R. Mildred Barker, brought to the Shakers at Alfred as a child of seven years in 1903, who today provides consecrated leadership to the little family at Sabbathday Lake.

Such is the nature of Shaker genealogy. Although family bloodlines may have little meaning in a celibate society, for the Shakers neither marry nor give in marriage, it is possible to trace a spiritual lineage for each Believer in the community today back to the founder of the faith herself. This unbroken chain of faith, Believer to Believer, is the real strength of Shakerism in Maine.

The community has also survived by virtue of its competent management of resources, as exemplified by the consolidation of the two communities in 1931. While other communities became encumbered by large dwellinghouses and shops that were no longer occupied, unused buildings at Sabbathday Lake were razed or moved after they had served their purpose. Thus the signs of disintegration, so evident in other Shaker villages, were nowhere to be found at Chosen Land. Credit for the preservation of the Society's physical properties and the careful stewardship of its resources in the first half of the twentieth century may be given to Eldress Elizabeth M. Noyes (1845–1925) and to Elders William Dumont (1851–1930) and Delmer C. Wilson (1873–1961), among others, who offered their time and talents, as well as a considerable store of ingenuity, to help the family persevere.

In speaking of Shaker survival in Maine, one is struck by what appears to be an almost stubborn adherence to the ways of the faith. While not fearing contact with the world, the Shakers at Sabbathday Lake tended to conserve their traditions. It is not generally known that other Shaker communities surviving into the twentieth century abandoned much of a heritage that had been hallowed by time. Only in Maine, for example, was the practice of regular community

Nineteenth- and early twentieth-century Shaker leaders (top row from left to right: Sister Aurelia Mace, Eldress Hester Ann Adams, Eldress Elizabeth Noyes; middle row left to right: Elder William Dumont, Elder Joseph Brackett; bottom: Elder Otis Sawyer)

Sister R. Mildred Barker, senior trustee and
spiritual leader of the Sabbathday Lake Shakers

Brother Wayne Smith with family pets, Shaker
Village "back row"

worship maintained. Such practices as the annual reading of the Shaker Covenant, the observance of the Annual Fast, and the celebration of special days in the Shaker calendar continued to be a feature of life only in the Maine bishopric. This dogged determination on the part of the Maine Believers seems to have provided a fuller context for living the Shaker life in an ever more complex world. The simple fact is that the Sabbathday Lake Shakers have survived. While other communities have been transformed into museum villages or converted to other uses, Sabbathday Lake is still a Shaker village and its members still live the Shaker life. Their beautiful village may have the qualities associated with a museum setting, but its twelve major buildings house a community that is active and alive.

Sometimes the Shakers appear shy or reticent when questioned about the size of their community. They often repeat a favorite aphorism of Mother Ann's. "If there is but one called out of a generation, and that soul is faithful, it will have to travail and bear for all its generation." Or, they may quote the biblical promise that the Lord is present where two or three are gathered together in His name (Matthew 18:20). They may also point out that Mother Ann brought only eight others with her on a fateful voyage from Liverpool in 1774. The persistent visitor, however, will soon discover that but eight Believers remain in a community that once housed one hundred and fifty or more. While some of these community members are aged, new life has been infused by the presence of several young Believers. Indeed, the average age of the members of the community is younger today than it has been in more than two decades. The new additions to the family have provided concrete evidence that there is a future for the Society. It is a time of great and expectant hopefulness at Sabbathday Lake.

Shaker Origins

THE FAITH ACCEPTED in the wilderness of late-eighteenth-century Thompson's Pond Plantation had its obscure beginnings fifty years earlier in the bleak industrial boroughs of Lancashire, England. In 1747, a small group of religious enthusiasts began to hold meetings under the leadership of James and Jane Wardley, tailors in Bolton on the Moors, near Manchester. Heirs to a long tradition of dissenting religion that drew many of its adherents from England's poor and disadvantaged classes, the members of the Wardleys' conventicle were deeply affected by a sense of God's immanence in a lost and sinful world. Some believe that the Wardleys were members of the Society of Friends who had come under the influence of the last of the French Prophets, Huguenot millenarians from southeastern France and their English converts, but a direct connection between their faith and that of either movement is uncertain.

Popular religious dissent in seventeenth- and eighteenth-century England was drawn to millennial speculation and prophecy. When the French Prophets arrived on English shores in the early eighteenth century following the revocation of the Edict of Nantes and the end of religious toleration in France, there were scores of loosely organized groups of nonconformists, each preaching its own brand of millenarian religion. Dissent was frequently a noisy affair, and Ranters, Muggletonians and Fifth Monarchists, among others, preached and prophesied of the near approach of the millennium, as they called their followers to personal salvation. In many of its manifestations, this tradition of popular religion was not unlike the frontier faith of the New England hill country a century later, a movement in which the Shakers were to play a notable role.

The Wardleys' faith imposed no creed or rules of worship; its adherents relied wholly on the prompting of the Holy Spirit. But if the society did not practice any established forms or rituals, its meetings were unrestrained and emotional gatherings, characterized by bold and vigorous preaching and the reception of visions and revelations that, to the faithful, seemed resonant with redeeming power.

Sometimes, after sitting awhile in silent meditation, they were seized with a mightly trembling under which *they would often express the indignation of God against all sin. At other times they were exercised with singing, shouting and leaping for joy at the near prospect of salvation. They were often exercised with great agitations of body and limbs, running and walking the floor, with a variety of signs and operations, and swiftly passing and repassing each other, like clouds agitated with a mighty wind. No human power could imitate the wonderful operations with which they were affected while under the influence of these spiritual signs. From these exercises, so strange in the eyes of mankind, they received the appellation of Shakers. . . .*

Mother Ann

THE SHAKERS, or Shaking Quakers as they were also called, might have been lost to history but for the reception into their numbers in September 1758 of a remarkable twenty-two-year-old woman, Ann Lees, the daughter of a blacksmith. It is to Ann (her surname in later Shaker usage was shortened to Lee) that the Shakers look as the founder of their faith. As we shall see, her name continues to be revered in the little village at Sabbathday Lake, and the oral and written traditions concerning her life and testimony remain among the guiding principles of its daily rounds. The story of her life is central to their story.

For all its importance to the Shakers, Ann's birth in 1736, probably in Manchester, is not recorded and its precise date has never been ascertained, although the tradition of the church holds it to be February 29. One of eight children, Ann was baptized in the Church of England in her sixth year. The family was poor; in common with other English children of the laboring classes, she suffered through a sad and difficult childhood of factory labor in Manchester's textile mills. From her earliest years, she was drawn to religion and to a sense of spiritual longing. Ann was among those who gathered to hear George Whitefield, the Methodist preacher, in his great outdoor meetings, and she was deeply impressed by his emphasis on the redeeming nature of faith in Christ. It was in the Wardley society, however, that Ann was to find a spiritual home, although she remained at least a nominal member of the Anglican communion.

According to Shaker tradition, Ann Lees preferred not to marry. It was only in her twenty-sixth year, four years after she entered the Wardley society, that she acceded to the wishes of her family and, on January 5, 1762, accepted the hand of Abraham Standerin (the name also appears as Stanley or Standley), a blacksmith like her father. After they were wed, Ann and Abraham resided in her father's home in Manchester, among the crowded and grim tenements of Toad Lane. The next several years saw the birth of Ann's four children, but this was not a happy time for her. Her daughter Elizabeth's burial in October 1766 is recorded in the registry of the Manchester cathedral. Another child may have lived to the age of six or seven years, but the others died even earlier in their young lives.

The period of her cohabitation with her husband was trying for Ann. After the death of her children, over whom she grieved, and at least one extremely difficult delivery that nearly ended in her death, she terminated marital relations with Abraham. "The man to whom I was married," she later recalled,

was very kind, according to nature; he would have been willing to pass through a flaming fire for my sake, if I would but live in the flesh with him, which I refused to do.

This determination on Ann's part, and her increasing willingness to voice her convictions, led to a direct breach in her relationship with her husband, who sought the intercession of the Anglican parish officials in an effort to win back her affection. This confrontation with husband and church marked the beginning of a major turning point in Ann's life. She fasted, deprived herself of sleep, and prayed and waited on the Spirit, seeking to discover the way to salvation. Devout Shakers were later to look back on this period as one of preparation for Ann, because she

was chosen not only to work out her own salvation, but to set the example of righteousness and mark out the line of self denial and the cross to her followers.

Any brief sketch of the childhood and marriage of Ann Lee tends to suggest a number of simplistic explanations for the development of the faith to which she was to devote her life. Deprivation and poverty, an unwanted marriage and the early deaths of her mother and young children, are offered as proof that her faith was a negative response or withdrawal from reality. For the Shakers of Sabbathday Lake, this kind of speculation misses the point. Tens of thousands experienced the utter degradation of English industrial life and surrendered to darkness and despair. Poverty, infant mortality and harsh working conditions were commonplace in eighteenth-century Manchester. The Shakers believe that Ann Lee, an unlettered millworker, transcended these hardships to discover a faith that offered salvation to a lost generation. Hers was a faith of hope.

Ann brought an invigorated sense of mission to the Wardley society. The movement was also strengthened by several members of modest means and property—John Townley, whose house in Cannon Street, Manchester, frequently served as a meeting place; John Hocknell of Cheshire, a Methodist; and John Partington of Mayortown, all of whom were able to provide at least some material support for the Society's work. As the Shakers became more open in their public testimony in the late 1760s and early 1770s, opposition to them mounted. There were direct and unpleasant confrontations with the civil and religious authorities, especially in the years 1772 and 1773; there was also more intense abuse from mobs.

The Shaker tradition is filled with stories that tell of the almost miraculous deliverance of these early Believers from the assault of their opponents. At various times, Ann herself is said to have been seized and beaten and stoned, escaping more often than not through what the faithful viewed as divine intervention, although once it was an unnamed "nobleman" who rescued her from the ravages of a crowd. Angered by Ann's blunt preaching, perhaps suspicious or fearful of the motives of the small group of Shakers, the people of Manchester seemed more than ready to express their opposition in violent acts, and

Shaker worship frequently was interrupted by stone throwing and the breaking of windows.

The Lees family itself was split over Shakerism. Ann's widowed father accepted the developing faith (although he was originally opposed to it), as did her brother William. But another brother joined a gang that seized Ann and tried to throw her from a "high loft building," probably the home of John Townley in Cannon Street. Perhaps he was among those who, on another occasion, burst into the Townley house, ascended the stairs to the third-floor garret where the Shakers worshipped, and assaulted them.

As lurid as the accounts drawn from recorded Shaker tradition appear, they cannot be dismissed as pious legend. On the contrary, the scant official proceedings available to us from Manchester seem to support their accuracy. In October 1772, according to the account books of Manchester's constable, the authorities were called upon to quell a mob "who were beginning to pull down the House of John Townley a Shaker." Obviously, the noisy exuberance of Shaker worship, sometimes held late into the night, won few friends for the Believers.

The previous July, the constable provided twenty-four persons with drafts of ale and a sixpence each for assisting in the arrest of Ann, her father and three other Shakers. Of the five, Ann and John Lees "were sentenced for an assault, to be imprisoned one month." This was not to be the Shakers' last unhappy confrontation with English justice. The constable's accounts record the cost of repairs necessary at the Lees home in Toad Lane in October 1772, when "a gang of Shakers lock't up there" were apprehended and Ann's brother, James, was arrested. On May 30, 1773, Ann was taken into custody again, this time for disturbances in the cathedral; at the following July quarter sessions of the court, she, John Townley, John Jackson and Betty Lees, all Shakers, were fined twenty pounds each

for going into Christ Church in Manchester, and there willfully and contemptuously in the Time of Divine Service disturbing the Congregation there assembled at Morning Prayer.

Ann's failure to pay the fine led to her confinement in the House of Correction, an old jail on the banks of the Irwell, known popularly as the Dungeon for the dark pit on its ground floor. Imprisonment had a profound effect on Ann:

In the midst of her sufferings and earnest cries to God, her soul was filled with divine light, and the mysteries of the spiritual world were brought clearly to her understanding. She saw the Lord Jesus Christ in his glory, who revealed to her the great object of her prayers, and fully satisfied all the desires of her soul. The most astonishing visions and divine manifestations were presented to her view in so clear and striking a manner, that the whole spiritual world seemed displayed before her.

When she was released from prison, Ann testified to the Shakers concerning the things revealed to her, that "no soul could follow Christ in regeneration while living in the works of generation." Ann appeared radiant and illuminated to the members of the Society, as one transfigured. In the eyes of the little group, she had overcome;

the candle of the Lord was in her hand, and . . . she was able by the light thereof, to search every heart and try every soul among them. From this time she was received and acknowledged,

according to an early Shaker account, "as the first visible leader of the Church of God upon earth."

Now known as Mother Ann to her followers, the blacksmith's daughter replaced the Wardleys as leader of the Society. As a result of her revelation in the House of Correction, the Shakers accepted celibacy in imitation of the life of Christ as a fundamental tenet of the then-developing faith.

The Shakers continued to worship in Manchester and nearby towns in late 1773 and early 1774, avoiding persecution by traveling at night. This was a period of "almost entire peace" for the group. The 22-year-old James Whittaker, who sustained Mother Ann in prison, began to take an active role in the life of the Society, but

Light through a window of the 1794 Meeting-house

there seemed to be little growth and perhaps some losses. Indeed, there is some evidence that the public preaching of the Believers ceased entirely.

Fear of stagnation may have led to the momentous decision, taken following a vision received by Whittaker, to leave England for America. At Mother Ann's request, John Hocknell secured passage for Ann and eight followers, including her brother William and the faithful James Whittaker, on the *Mariah*, and the little band embarked from Liverpool in May 1774.

Also aboard was Abraham Standerin, Ann's husband, who then professed to have accepted her faith.

Arrival in America

THE SHAKERS ARRIVED in New York harbor on August 6, 1774, two months and eighteen days after leaving Liverpool. Although they must have been relieved to catch their first glimpse of land, they could not have known what lay ahead for them. Each of them had left behind family members and friends with whom their lives had been closely connected in the little church. Although the Hocknells and John Partington and his children would yet join their brethren in America, the rest of the English Shakers pass from history.

The Shakers were strangers in the provincial port town of New York, and securing a livelihood and a place to lodge was an immediate concern. Ann and Abraham were able to find a home and employment with a blacksmith and his wife on Queen Street, now known as Pearl Street, in lower Manhattan. Legend has it that on the day of their arrival, Ann walked resolutely to the home of the blacksmith and, addressing his wife by name, announced that she had been "commissioned of the Almighty God to preach the everlasting Gospel to America," and that an angel had commanded her to take up residence there. Abraham was employed as a blacksmith, while Ann kept house. She counseled the other Shakers to find employment where they could. According to tradition, they conferred with local Quakers and were advised to go upstate to Albany, where inexpensive land was available. In Albany, William Lee secured employment as a blacksmith, and James Whittaker as a weaver. In 1775, John Hocknell leased land consisting of about two hundred acres from the Van Rensselaers in what was then known as Niskayuna, located in the Manor Renselaerwyck not far from Albany. Ann also traveled to Albany several times, but without Abraham. After having nursed him through an illness, she was abandoned by her husband, who returned to the ways of the world. After working as a housekeeper and laundress for two years, she joined the others at Niskayuna in 1776.

If the little group experienced joy in coming together after two years of separation, it must have been tempered by an awareness of the extreme harshness of their surroundings. The land leased by Hocknell was located within a dense forest through which the Scherluyn Creek ran an uncertain and winding course. Pools of standing water and huge bogs with wild grasses and weeds abounded, and the land seemed to offer little promise as a stable or permanent home for the Believers. Very much in the familiar tradition of other pioneering endeavors in North America, however, the Shakers dug in their heels and began to clear the land for farming, and to render the wilderness more hospitable.

It was not until some years later that Mother

A variety of traditional
crafts continues
to be practiced today.

Skeins of yarn and woodenware in Sisters Shop.

Shaker "tape loom" and flax wheel on exhibition at Sabbathday Lake museum (formerly ministry apartments, 1794 Meetinghouse)

Ann and her followers publicly proclaimed their message. In March 1780, the visit of two participants in the "New Light" revival that had swept the countryside along the New York–Massachusetts border southeast of Albany the previous year, signaled a new opening. In towns like New Lebanon, New York, and Hancock, Massachusetts, gospel fires burned rampantly, as preachers called the people to repent before the Second Coming of Christ in glory. By the end of 1779, however, the fires were not burning as brightly, and many of the participants in the revival became disaffected or disillusioned. The two New Light travelers spoke with Mother Ann about the failure of the revival and, according to the traditional stories, were astonished when she testified that it was not necessary to wait any longer for the Second Coming. Christ had appeared again, she assured them. "If you are ever saved by Christ, it must be by walking as he walked." She explained that by confession and turning away from the ways of the world, the truly repentant creates a dwelling place for the Spirit of Christ. The two visitors returned to New Lebanon and repeated what they had heard to the leaders of the revival, one of whom was Joseph Meacham, a Baptist preacher from Enfield, Connecticut. Before long, Meacham and many of his New Light associates had been converted. Father Joseph, as he would be called, would have a major role in helping spread the Shaker message and in providing structure and leadership to the nascent church.

Within the next few years, as the result of a difficult but courageous itinerant ministry led by Mother Ann, her brother William, James Whittaker, and Joseph Meacham, the faith spread rapidly. In addition to those at New Lebanon, New York (which would become the seat of the central ministry of the church), and Niskayuna or Watervliet, New York, (the site of the original Shaker settlement near Albany), Shaker missionaries gathered groups of Believers at Hancock, Tyringham, Harvard and Shirley, Massachusetts; Enfield, Connecticut; Enfield and Canterbury, New Hampshire; and Alfred and Thompson's Pond Plantation (New Gloucester), Maine.

The Opening of the Testimony in Thompson's Pond Plantation

IN NOVEMBER 1782, three Shaker missionaries from Gorham, Maine, visited New Gloucester and neighboring Thompson's Pond Plantation and Bakerstown to preach among people caught up in the frontier religious revival then sweeping through much of northern New England. The hundreds of settlers pouring into the frontier regions surrounding such towns as New Gloucester brought with them a democratic spirit and a heightened sense of personal autonomy. They were drawn to a radical evangelical faith that challenged established Congregationalism, seeking the separation of church and state and rejecting the dour Calvinism of the old religion. For these frontier sectarians, a faith that offered salvation on the basis of individual choice (or "free grace," as it was called) was preferable to the cold doctrines of predestination and election. The revivalists became known as "New Lights," "Merry Dancers," or "Come-Outers." Revival meetings were lengthy, emotional affairs, characterized by the ecstatic acceptance of charismatic gifts and the preaching of the imminent approach of the Second Coming. Among the sectarian leaders was Benjamin Randall of New Durham, New Hampshire, who visited New Gloucester in July 1782 and succeeded in converting a large group of revivalists to his Freewill Baptist faith. It was to these people that Elisha Pote, Nathan Freeman and Joseph Stone, the three Shaker emissaries from Gorham, came in the autumn of the same year to preach the Gospel of Christ's Second Appearing.

The Shakers found in the Freewill Baptists a fertile field for their own preaching. Theirs was even a more radical faith than that of Randall's followers. It taught the fulfillment of the Second Coming as a reality in the lives of Believers, and sought to provide a practical means of living out the principles of the apostolic church as de-

Shaker oval boxes

From the Ministry's apartments, meetinghouse

Shaker Village at Sabbathday Lake in winter (left to right: Boys' Shop, office woodshed, Trustees' Office)

scribed in the New Testament. Shaker inroads into the membership of Freewill Baptist congregations had already been successful in New Hampshire and elsewhere in Maine. In January 1783, the clerk of the Freewill Baptist congregation in Loudon and Canterbury, New Hampshire, wrote to Randall and the other church leaders in New Durham "with a sorrowful heart" to inform them of his group's sad state.

If I mistake not, all of our Elders and Deacons have left us and joined the Shaking Quakers (so called), and with them a great part of the church. Most of the rest seem to be in a cold, dull, melancholy state.

Continuing Shaker successes in the ferment of frontier revivalism led to the decision taken by the Freewill Baptist Quarterly Meeting in 1784 to observe a day of fasting and prayer against the Shaker "delusion."

It is sometimes difficult to understand how ordinary people could become so deeply involved in questions of church doctrine and practice. Frontier revival was not simply a question of rampant emotionalism. Successful preachers had to present sound arguments that were equal to the intellectual challenges of their audiences. To be sure, deeply felt concerns for personal salvation prompted great fervor and passion in the hill country, but religious ideas absorbed the intellects of these country folk just as strongly.

The Shakers held meetings that first autumn of 1782 in the house of Gowen Wilson, Senior. Elder Elisha Pote, whose "reasonings were clear and convincing" and "voice mild and persuasive," led the preaching. Elder Otis Sawyer, for many years first elder in the Maine ministry, preserved this description of that first Shaker meeting at Gowen Wilson's farm:

After preaching they sang and went forth in the dance with much power. After singing and laboring one song, they gave liberty for any one to unite with them who wished to, when Dorothy Pote and Mary Merrill were simultaneously inspired by the power of God, their bodies mightily agitated and they turned swiftly round like tops for the space of one hour. They both received faith, and with many others . . . confessed their sins and were baptized by the spiritual Jordan . . .

Dorothy Pote and Mary Merrill were the first Believers gathered in Thompson's Pond Plantation by Elder Elisha and his companions from Gorham. Before long, several large families joined them, including a number from nearby Bakerstown (later called Poland) and from as far away as Buckfield. In their efforts to win converts to the cause, Shaker missionaries often followed the paths taken by their kinsmen and neighbors. Among these friends and relatives, they knew they would find a welcome as well as a place to lodge, and to preach. Buckfield, for example, had been settled by New Gloucester folk in 1777. Among its first residents were the Thurlows and the Cushmans, who were related by marriage to the Ring family of Bakerstown. All would become Shakers. Indeed, it was the reception into the church of large natural families, often consisting of several generations of husbands, wives and children, that assured its early success. At Sabbathday Lake, for example, twenty-four members of the Briggs family became Shakers; twenty-nine members of the Holmes family; the Merrill family, the largest of them all, accounted for thirty-two converts. By 1784, one hundred eighty-four Shakers had been gathered, including members of the Wilson, Pote and other families. The local leadership consisted of Edmund Merrill and Joseph Briggs, elder brethren, and Elizabeth Thurlow and Mercy Holmes as elder sisters.

The first Shakers of Thompson's Pond Plantation continued to live on their own farms, but many found a spiritual home in the North Parish of Sanford, forty-five miles to the south. There, a group of Believers gathered on the farm of Benjamin Barnes, whose lands adjoining Massabesic Lake were soon to be the site of the Alfred Shaker Society. The gathering at Sanford North Parish was the result of the conversion of John Cotton—the first Believer in the District of Maine.

John Cotton Accepts Shakerism

JOHN COTTON was one of many caught up in the revival sweeping across northern New England. A New Light Christian, he persevered in the faith despite considerable opposition to his "disorderly" behavior. He and his friend, John Barnes, interrupted Congregationalist meetings "to such a degree that it became necessary to take them out and fasten them with ropes to a tree." The two "Merry Dancers" used to don strange garb and "hoot at the devil" or scream "woe! woe!! woe!!!" so loudly that the words "were audible in the stillness of the evening nearly the distance of one mile."

Cotton met Benjamin Randall in 1780, during the Freewill Baptist preacher's first visit to Maine, and was drawn to Randall's convictions. In 1781, while on a journey westward through New Hampshire to Vermont, where he intended to find a home for himself and his wife, Eleanor, he tarried at Enfield, another New Light center. Among the local brethren was James Jewett, who had accepted the Shaker faith from the preaching of Believers from New Lebanon, New York, and had become an eloquent exponent of the cause himself. He and Cotton entered into long conversations about the nature of salvation and the Kingdom of Heaven. Cotton recorded the remarkable occurrences that followed one of these conversations.

The power of God came upon me, filling my soul and controlling my whole being. It raised me from my chair, and under its influence I turned around, swiftly, for the space of half an hour. The door of the house was open. I was whirled through the doorway, into the yard among stones and stumps, down to the shore of Mascoma Lake, some rods distant. On reaching the shore of the lake that same power that led me to the water whirled me back again in like manner, and I found myself in the same chair that I had been taken from. This was a seal to my faith and baptism of the Holy Spirit, and I promised to obey it to the end of my days.

John Cotton's conversion experience parallels that of many new Believers. We have already seen how Dorothy Pote and Mary Merrill "turned swiftly round like tops" for an hour when they received the Gospel in the wilderness of Sabbathday Pond in 1782. However strange these stories may appear to us, the power of the new faith in the experience of these Believers was life-changing then and remains so now. For John Cotton, it meant abandoning plans to settle in Vermont. He quickly turned back east to tell his family and friends what he had heard and seen in Enfield.

Upon his return home, John Cotton brought news of the Gospel of Christ's Second Appearing to his New Light brethren in Sanford North Parish and Gorham. Within one day of his return, John and Sarah Barnes had become Believers. Soon others joined them. That summer, James Jewett, together with Elder Ebenezer Cooley, a Shaker teacher from New Lebanon, New York, and Eliphalet Comstock of Hancock, Massachusetts, arrived to encourage the new Believers in their faith. Accompanied by John Cotton and John Barnes, they held meetings not only in Alfred and Gorham, but in Lyman, Waterborough and Windham, and many souls were drawn into the Shaker fold.

Ministry and Mission

WHEN THE SHAKERS first spread their message in the District of Maine, Mother Ann Lee, the founder of the faith, was still ministering to her flock in New York and Massachusetts and gathering new souls to the cause.

During her ministry, she instructed, counseled and reproved the Believers in her characteristic straightforward way. These teachings, which were published after her death in several collections of *Testimonies*, say much about Mother Ann's simple wisdom and charismatic personality. Throughout their generations, the Shakers have treasured them.

From the Precepts of Mother Ann

ON CLEANLINESS

Lucy Bishop was once scrubbing a room; and Mother Ann came in and said, "Clean your room well; for good spirits will not live where there is dirt. There is no dirt in heaven."

ON TEMPORAL ECONOMY

While Mother Ann was at Petersham [Massachusetts] in the summer of 1783, she took an opportunity to instruct some of the heads of families, who were there, concerning temporal economy; and admonished them against some of their costly and extravagant furniture, saying, "Never put on silver spoons, nor table

cloths for me; but let your table be clean enough to eat from without cloths, and if you do not know what to do with them, give them to the poor."

ON THE FEAR OF GOD

At Watervliet [New York], Mother spoke to a number of Believers as follows; "You ought to fear God, in all you do, for God's eyes are upon you. You ought to go in and out in the fear of God, and open and shut doors carefully, and make no unnecessary noise. You must be faithful with your hands, that you may have something to give the poor; and walk ye uprightly like men of God."

ON CHARITY

At Nathan Goodrich's in Hancock, Mother Ann spoke to the people concerning charity to the poor, and

Towel and chair in brethren's waiting room, Central Brick Dwelling

said, "If I owned the whole world, I would turn it all into joyfulness; I would not say to the poor 'Be ye warmed and be ye clothed,' without giving them the wherewithal to do it."

ON WORK

A certain young man came to Mother with some peach and plum stones in his hand, and asked her if he might plant them. "Yea," answered Mother, "do all your work as though you had a thousand years to live, and as you would if you knew you must die tomorrow."

Mother Ann never visited Maine, but several of the northern Believers traveled to see her. John Cotton and three of the brethren saw Mother and the first Elders at Harvard, Massachusetts, in June 1783, at the time she and the other leaders of the church were set upon by a mob in an incident recalled to this day. After tying Father James Whittaker to a tree and cruelly beating him, the mob seized Mother Ann's brother, William Lee, "but he chose to kneel down and be whipped, therefore they did not tie him; but began to whip him as he stood on his knees." Notwithstanding the severity of his own beating, Father James immediately leaped upon William's back and a Shaker sister, Bethiah Willard, and others followed his example. They were all "inhumanly beaten without mercy." Later the Shakers marked the spot where Father James was beaten with a stone monument. It became the custom of Shakers passing the site to place a stone there. The Believers of Chosen Land have continued the practice. The monument, which remains in place to this day, contains the stark and simple inscription, "On this spot a Shaker was whiped [sic] by a mob for religious views in 1783."

After assisting in Mother Ann's four-year public ministry, her brother, William, died on July 21, 1784, at the age of forty-five years. The memory of Father William is revered among Believers. So ardently did he labor for the upbuilding of the church that he is referred to as an "apostle in sufferings." Many memories of his character are preserved in church chronicles.

He often expressed his great love for the Brethren and Sisters. At one time, in Ashfield [Massachusetts] . . . he manifested his love to the Brethren and Sisters, in the following words, "I love you so well that I should be willing to give you every gift of God that I have, and then set out anew, to labor for more."

When great numbers of the Believers came to the Church to see them, he would often meet them at the door and say, "Come in, Brethren and Sisters, come in;—we have but little room in our house, but we have a great of room in our hearts."

Ann Lee was very much affected by the death of her brother. Weakened by four years of intensive toil, she felt her own life was coming to an end. On September 8, 1784, a little more than ten years after her arrival in America, she said to those with her at Niskayuna, "I see Brother William, coming in a golden chariot, to take me home." She died shortly thereafter at the age of forty-eight.

OBITUARY

Departed this life at Nisquenia, . . . Mrs. Lee, known by the appellation of the Elect Lady or Mother of Zion, and head of that people called Shakers. Her funeral is to be attended this day.
Albany Gazette
September 9, 1784

A traditional story of the Shakers concerns the last days of Ann Lee. In August 1784, a group of twenty-five Believers from Sabbathday Pond and Alfred made a pilgrimage to the upstate New York settlement of Niskayuna, where Ann Lee and her followers from England had established a home in 1776. It was near the end of Mother Ann's life and she was frail, but she made an effort to see each of the pilgrims. James Merrill, Senior, was then over seventy years of age, and Mother was moved that one so aged should have undertaken such an arduous trip. Only forty-eight years of age herself, she called him her "white headed little boy," and he received a "special gift of blessing" from her. In addition to visiting with Mother Ann, the group from Maine attended "many powerful meetings" and became more thoroughly imbued with the spirit of the faith.

On the way home in early September, their little sailing vessel encountered a severe storm and seemed in danger of being lost. At the height of the weather's fury, Sister Dana Thoms saw a vision of Mother Ann. It was a story the Shakers often recall. Mother "looked calmly and smilingly upon her and with uplifted hands breathed peace to the troubled sea." According to the tale, the storm soon subsided. When the Believers disembarked at Portland harbor, they learned that Ann Lee had died on September 8, 1784, between the hours of twelve and one in the morning, six hours before Sister Dana saw her calming the seas.

Father James Whittaker led the Society for three years until his own death on July 20, 1787. The mantle of leadership then fell on the capable shoulders of Joseph Meacham, who would preside over the organization of the church in "Gospel Order," the Shaker system of church government and social and economic association.

Meacham conceived of a three-court "family" system in which Believers would be grouped according to their "conditions of travel in the Gospel." In this arrangement, the inner "court" or family, generally called the Church Family, was to be composed only of fully committed Believers, those willing to contribute all to the common good. A second family, or junior order, was to be reserved for individuals with some ties to the world, while the gathering or novitiate family would receive inquirers and help them to a fuller acceptance of Shakerism. Each family was to be autonomous, with separate economic affairs, and to consist of a mere handful to a hundred or more members.

Meacham established the leadership principle in the United Society, as well. Presiding over each family would be a "lot" or order of elders, composed of two brethren and two sisters. These four elders would be responsible to the ministry of the bishopric, generally composed of all the Shaker societies in a single state. The order of the ministry of the bishopric was also to be composed of two elders and two eldresses, who in turn would be responsible to the central or parent Ministry at New Lebanon, New York. The first ministry of the bishopric of Maine consisted of Father John Barnes, Mother Sarah Kendall, and their associates, Robert McFarland and Lucy Prescott.

Father Joseph appointed an accomplished and deeply consecrated Shaker sister, Lucy Wright, to serve in the central ministry with him. After Father Joseph's death on August 16, 1796, Mother Lucy, as first eldress, presided over the period of the church's greatest growth and development until she herself died in 1821. During Mother Lucy's ministry, new Shaker societies were gathered at Union Village and Watervliet, Ohio; Pleasant Hill and South Union, Kentucky; and West Union, Indiana. Within a few years after her death, the Shakers organized three additional communities, at North Union and Whitewater, Ohio, and Sodus Bay, New York (later moved to Groveland, New York).

Gathering in Gospel Order

IN THE EARLIEST DAYS of the Church in Maine, regular meetings for worship were held in the homes and barns of Believers. But in the summer of 1786, the Shakers at Alfred built their first crude meetinghouse. Then, in March 1793, the church leadership dispatched the master builder Brother Moses Johnson of Enfield, New Hampshire, to supervise the construction of a new, more permanent meetinghouse for the Alfred community. The first meetinghouse Brother Moses constructed was at New Lebanon in 1785–6. It served as a model for all the rest, its distinctive gambrel roof setting it apart from other community buildings. By the time he arrived at Alfred, the brethren had already cut and sawed the timber for it. The Alfred meetinghouse was dedicated in 1793, although the interior was not finished until the following year.

The earliest joint efforts at building among the Shakers of Sabbathday Pond were the construction of a gristmill in 1786 and a sawmill in 1796, the tall pines providing the foundation of an enterprise that would be important in the economic life of the Village for the next 150 years. After the formal organization of the Shaker Society there on April 19, 1794, according to the principles of Gospel Order, the local brethren began building in earnest. In June, Moses Johnson, who by then had completed the Alfred meetinghouse, came to Sabbathday Pond to help the brethren frame their house of worship.

The meetinghouse was raised on June 14, 1794, in reverent silence. It is the oldest remaining major structure in the Village (a garden shed is older) and continues to serve the Shakers as a place of praise and devotion. But for a signpost on the lawn in front of it, its purpose would not be evident. Only the Shakers adapted the New England style of gambrel-roofed building for their churches, and no steeple or religious symbol adorns it. In size, the structure is forty-four feet, seven inches long by thirty-two feet, seven inches wide, not including a small stair wing

added in 1839. Its two upper floors served as living quarters for the ministry until the nearby Ministry's Shop was built. It has a gentle quality of grace and dignity about it, perhaps from the pleasant symmetry of its design. It is also a marvel of engineering. Although its meeting room occupies the entire first floor except for the stair wing, no columns interrupt the openness of the large room. Twelve boxed and braced beams, running across the width of the ceiling, support the upper part of the structure. It was completed and ready for use on Christmas Day, 1794.

At the end of the nineteenth century, Sister Aurelia Mace recorded her first impressions of the interior of the meetinghouse as a young girl in 1842.

I once heard James Wakefield sing a beautiful song in one of our meetings. He was a very white, clean

"World's people's" benches, 1794 Meetinghouse

looking brother and the music rolled from his lips in volumes.

It was the first time I ever saw the inside of the meetinghouse. So you see I was very young. The blue wood work over head and the white ceiling between, the blue walls [wainscoting] and white floor, all seemed wonderful and the place was heaven to me.

The same sentiments are often voiced by today's family of Believers and those who worship with them in the old church. The original deep, warm, blue-green color is still there, too. Indeed, none of the interior woodwork—wainscoting, beams, or the two long, parallel rows of pegboard encircling the room—have been repainted since 1794.

The Shaker preference for self-sufficiency was evident, even as early as 1794, in the building of the meetinghouse. The brethren made the 20,000 bricks required for each of the building's two chimneys near the foot of Sabbathday Pond. Even the nails used in the meetinghouse's construction were Shaker-made.

The year following the completion of their house of worship, the Believers erected a large frame dwellinghouse, its two front doors facing the two front doors of the meetinghouse across the way. With a home for its members, the beginning of an economic base in its sawmill and in agriculture, and a place for Believers to practice their faith in the song and dance of their worship, Shaker Village had been established. The Village would continue to grow during the early nineteenth century. By 1814, the Believers had constructed twelve buildings in addition to the meetinghouse and central dwelling that were used for a variety of sisters' and brethren's trades. Several structures remained from the earlier pre-Shaker period, too, and were converted to community use. Soon, two separate "families" of Believers would join the one already established in Shaker Village, expanding the community even further.

As we have seen, when John Cotton returned home from Vermont in 1781, he brought news of his conversion to New Light friends in Gorham, Maine, many of whom were drawn to the faith. In 1807, under the leadership of the Shakers at

Alfred, a community was established in Gorham on the farms of Barnabas Bangs and Joseph Brackett, as well as on nearby properties, and a dwellinghouse and other structures were built to house approximately sixty Believers. For reasons that remain unclear, the leadership of the Society determined to transfer this family to the vicinity of the New Gloucester community and, in 1819, the group moved to Poland Hill, about one mile north of the existing village.

The Shakers established a third family in 1820, located in the town of Poland about midway between the upper and lower communities, on the Chipman Road. They purchased an eighteenth-century structure known locally as the Square House, "a plain old fashioned four roofed building" that had once served the locality as a "house of entertainment," for the use of the family, but the group was not to survive long.

Mother's Work

IN LATE 1837 at the Shaker community at Watervliet, New York, the entire Society embarked on a period of intense involvement with spiritual phenomena unlike any other in its history. During this period, known as the Era of Mother's Work, or the Era of Manifestations, which lasted with varying intensity from place to place for fifteen or twenty years, inspiration was a daily phenomenon in the villages. The faithful believed that many of the departed saints of Shaker history, Mother Ann and the first elders among them, as well as a host of heavenly figures and angels, were walking among them, helping them to cleave more closely to the gospel way. Inspired "instruments" brought messages of comfort and love. The more gifted among the visionists received strangely beautiful and affecting songs of encouragement and consolation, many of which survive in the oral tradition at Sabbathday Lake. As the Era of Mother's Work followed a period of loss and falling away in the communities, the leadership saw in the manifestations a call from Heaven to return to the fundamentals of the faith.

Shaker "gift drawing" by Polly Collins. "A gift from Mother Ann to Eldress Eunice, August 1859." Watercolor and ink on paper

Shaker scribes recorded thousands of visions before the era came to an end. The visions were frequently in the form of spiritual "gifts," and had a wonderful childlike quality about them. At Sabbathday Lake, those older members of the community who had participated in the manifestations, continued to receive "gifts" well after the end of the era, as this entry from the official "Church Record" indicates.

MAY 3, 1885. SABBATH

[At meeting] Mother Anne Hurd came with a little present. A Ball of Gold Thread, each little good deed will add to its beauty she said. You can keep winding and winding said she and this ball will continue to brighten until it shall look like pure gold. And it—will be the Gold of Truth, this will stand the Gospel fire.

During the Era of Mother's Work, the Shakers set aside special "feast grounds" in each community where they conducted elaborate rituals around monuments symbolizing spiritual fountains. Each "fountain stone" was inscribed with verses received by inspiration; the Believers developed some of their most intricate and moving dance or marching forms during the era, as well. In a period marked by its otherworldliness, each community received a spiritual name. At Sabbathday Lake, it was Chosen Land.

We have seen the community come together in gospel order, in pursuit of a vision. We know that its members had accepted a radical religion brought from England by Mother Ann Lee in 1774. But we cannot understand the ways marked out for Believers two hundred years ago, or walk the paths of their village today without considering the nature of their faith. It, more than anything else, has shaped their lives.

Brother Theodore E. Johnson

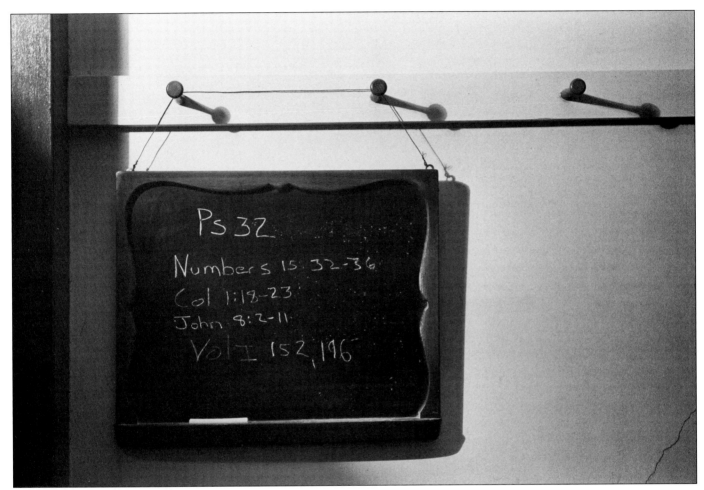

Blackboard in vestibule of Central Brick Dwelling. Biblical readings and lessons and "set songs" for Sabbath meeting are posted

The Nature of the Shaker Faith

THE FAITH BROUGHT to Thompson's Pond Plantation was not a fully elaborated doctrinal system. Not until the early nineteenth century would Shaker religious thinkers like Benjamin Seth Youngs and John Dunlavy begin to grapple with the problems of theology. However, certain basic assumptions were always clear, and Father Joseph Meacham, the church's first American-born leader, enunciated these in *A Concise Statement of the Principles of the Only True Church According to the Gospel of the Present Appearance of Christ*. Printed in Bennington, Vermont in 1790, this was the Society's first publication. These early Believers taught that God's work in history is progressive, having been manifested in four successive dispensations of grace from the beginning of time. The last of these, which began in Lancashire in 1747 in the meetings of the Wardley Society, was the Second Appearing of Christ as an indwelling and sanctifying reality in the lives of Believers. The Shakers taught that, by accepting the yoke of the Kingdom of Heaven, the Believer may find regenerating deliverance from sin and become fully alive in God. This may be accomplished by a sincere confession of all transgressions and a denial of worldly lust. In its essentials, this is the Shaker faith.

In stressing confession and chastity, Mother Ann and the first elders sought to restore the practices of the New Testament church. They taught that to follow Christ in the Regeneration, the Believer must give up the works of generation. They quoted Jesus in the Gospel according to St. Luke (20:34–35) that

The children of this world marry, and are given in marriage: But they which shall be accounted worthy to obtain that world, and the resurrection from the dead, neither marry nor are given in marriage.

Beyond these basic assumptions, which are immutable, the Shakers hold that their faith is a creative, evolving force, active in their lives and not subject to facile or dogmatic formulation. As early as 1812–13, in his preface to *Millennial Praises*, the Society's first printed hymnal, Seth Youngs Wells, an important early leader of the church, argued against attempts to confine Shaker faith to any system of words.

It is not expected that the people of God will ever be confined, in their mode of worship, to any particular set of hymns, or any other regular system of words—for words are but the signs of our ideas, and of course, must vary as the ideas increase with the increasing work of God . . . As the work of regeneration is an increasing work, and as there can be no end of the increase of Christ's government and Kingdom; so all that his people have to do is, to keep in the increasing work of God, and unite whatever changes that increase may lead to, which, to the truly faithful, will be a continual travel from grace to grace, and from glory to glory . . .

Doctrines of the Church

IN THE EXCERPT from *Millennial Praises*, Brother Seth stressed the progressive or processual nature of Shaker faith. This is not to suggest, however, that the religious tradition of the church is so uncertain or subject to change that there is not a received body of belief to which all Believers assent. The Shakers accept the Bible, for example, as an authentic expression of the word of God, although they do not approach it from a "fundamentalist" standpoint. According to the Shaker view, divine revelation is not confined to the pages of the Bible, but all religious ideas must be judged against its authority. It is a popular misconception that the Shakers have a Bible of their own or a body of literature equivalent to it. On the contrary, they place great emphasis on the Holy Scriptures. Regular Bible study continues to this day as a feature of Shaker life at Sabbathday Lake.

As Shaker religious thinkers underwent their own conversion experiences and "travel in the Gospel," they received insights into the nature of a faith they previously had understood only experientially. One of the most important of these developing ideas was the principle that the one God is manifest as both Father and Mother, an idea that was consistent with the biblical account of man's creation: "So God created man in his own image . . . male and female . . ." (Genesis 1:27). This has had far-reaching effects in Shaker life and community organization, allowing women to enjoy equality with men in the leadership of the church.

An extension of this idea, held by many Shakers, and fully elaborated by the early nineteenth century, is that as Jesus is the firstborn Son of God, so Ann Lee is his Daughter. According to this view Ann, during her imprisonment in England, received from God the same anointing that Jesus did when he was baptized in the Jordan. This allowed her to mark out the way of salvation for women, as Jesus did for men. Other Believers rejected this view. It is accurate to state, however, that all Shakers recognize Ann Lee as Mother in Christ. As Christ appeared a second time in her life and ministry, they believe, he will enter the hearts of all men and women who follow him in regeneration. For Believers, that is the meaning of Christ's Second Appearing.

As the Shakers came together as a church, they began to interpret New Testament thought more radically than other Christians. In order to maintain the sanctifying grace of Christ's indwelling, they taught, a measure of separation from the "world" was necessary; otherwise the Believer risked being drawn back into the world. The application of this idea would set Believers apart as a "peculiar" folk. Although living in community was not a necessary concomitant to the principle of separation, it was a pragmatic extension of the idea. The communal form of living finds authority in the practice of the early Christian church, as recorded in the Acts of the Apostles (4:32).

And the multitude of them that believed were of one heart and of one soul; neither said any of them that any of the things which he possessed was his own; but they had all things common.

In keeping with this idea, fully committed Believers (those entering the "inner court" of Father Joseph's family system) donated all their worldly possessions to the church. The church, on its part, agreed to provide for the needs of the Believer.

Their unity as a "separate" people and the central emphasis of their belief were emphasized by the Shakers in the name they chose for their church. It was the United Society of Believers in Christ's Second Appearing.

Another radical application of New Testament teaching, which the Shakers hold in common with other "peace" churches, is their witness against violence. The Shakers are pacifists; they do not participate in war, a fact that won them few friends during the American Revolution.

Very early in their history, the Shakers developed the worship patterns that would give their religious meetings a distinctive cast. The involuntary, ecstatic "shaking," from which Believers received their name, was ritualized into intricate dances or marches, and all women and men were invited to participate in "testifying" in meeting, as the spirit moved them. Of course, this meant that Shaker leaders had a difficult burden, especially in the early, frontier days, to transform religious excitement into genuine revival, so that in their worship the new Believers could obtain a true anointing of the Spirit. In an entry in her commonplace book, Sister Aurelia G. Mace, with tongue in cheek, described the problem that confronted Elder Ebenezer Cooley, an early Shaker preacher, when he held a meeting at Thompson's Pond Plantation in the infant days of the church. It seems that a certain Believer, by the name of Mehitable Winship Stinchfield, loved to preach, and as Sister Aurelia records it, was "radical in her expression." Elder Ebenezer asked all who were present to speak a few words of faith, and Mehitable, as the story goes, "could hardly wait her turn." When finally she was able to speak, "[t]hese were her words, spoken with a vim."

"I defy a whole army of men laden with lust," she said, "to defile my soul. It would take as much to

destroy my faith as it would to dethrone the great King of Zion."

Father Cooley checked her and said, "Woman, you don't know what you are saying."

Entry into the life of regeneration, according to the Shaker view, must be preceded by a true and contrite confession of all previous sin, stated before God in the presence of a witness. This is in accordance with the New Testament teaching that believers should "confess your faults one to another, and pray for one another, that ye may be healed (James 5:16)." The importance of confession, or "opening the mind," as the Shakers call it, cannot be overstated. The Shakers teach that in the process of confession, "releasement" follows, and the soul is rendered a fit place for the Indwelling Presence. Brother Granville Merrill, who would earn an important place in the history of the New Gloucester church entered the Society after working as a hired laborer for the Shakers in the 1860s. Sister Aurelia has left an account of his first confession.

He made his first confession in the presence of Alonzo Gilman, who was at that time Novitiate Elder. As Granville's home was in the lower village, he was one mile away from where Elder Alonzo was stationed at Poland Hill.

One day he went up to do this momentous work. Elder Alonzo happened at that tiime to be very busily engaged in hand labor, and could not attend to him. The burden did not fall from his shoulders like that of Bunyan's Pilgrim. He had to take it back home and wait for another opportunity. He went up the next day and again found Elder Alonzo too busy to give him attention. So he brought the burden back. In two or three days he went up the third time and found Elder Alonzo prepared, and the burden fell from his shoulders. He carried it up that steep hill to the foot of the cross three times, but the releasement was to him a sure reward.

It was only temporal labor that hindered Alonzo from attending to that most sacred duty. That was not right. The spiritual should always come first. But the trial did not hurt Granville.

A distinctive feature of Shaker belief is its otherworldliness. For the faithful of the church, the "resurrection state," as the Shakers call it, may begin in the here and now. But if the reality of the Indwelling Presence hallows the life of Believers in *this* world, it also points to a continuum with the *other* world, the invisible Kingdom of Heaven. In their daily rounds, in work as well as in worship, devout Shakers retain a certain sense of the nearness of a world of spirit as real to them, perhaps, as the material world is to the rest of us. This spiritual sensibility, which was particularly marked in the ministry of Mother Ann, has had a significant impact not only on the development of Shaker thought but on the folklore, music and arts of the people.

A story that comes down to us from the Shaker community at Mount Lebanon, New York, illustrates this sense of otherworldliness. It was recorded by Eldress Anna White and Sister Leila S. Taylor in their history of the movement, *Shakerism: Its Meaning and Message,* which was published in 1904.

MEETING A SPIRIT ARMY

In the summer of 1902, Sister Matilda Reed . . . passed to the spirit land from the Church Family, at Mount Lebanon. A member of the Society since early childhood, an Eldress in the Family for many years, she had been active and devoted during the greater part of the nineteenth century. The morning after her departure, Eldress Anna White was going on an errand to the Church office. She says: "I was enjoying the morning walk . . . and felt nothing uncommon until I had passed the large elm tree, where the two roads merge into one. Here a flood of life met me . . . there were whole congregations, like armies. It was like meeting a great mountain. The street was alive . . . I recognized [many] that I knew . . . I felt their greeting, and all the while I was saying, 'what does this mean?' "

"Entering the office, I said to the Sisters: 'Do you know how many are treading our streets to-day?' Sister Emma Neale replied, at once, 'Yea, I should think so! Sister Matilda will have a heavenly escort.' "

Growth and Decline

BY THE TIME they reached their greatest numerical strength in the 1830s, the Shakers, some five thousand strong, had achieved a degree of public acceptance, and even admiration. Indeed, their neat, efficient, self-contained agricultural/industrial villages became magnets to the utopian socialists and intellectuals of the day, who saw the Shakers' success as a validation of their own programs for the radical reshaping of society.

However, a slow but unremitting disintegration that began to affect the Shaker communities following the Civil War, accelerated with the advent of the twentieth century. Shaker life continued with remarkable robustness in the northern New England communities, but most of the few surviving villages were places of quiet streets and near-empty dwellinghouses and shops, where older Shakers seemed content to reflect upon events of earlier days, while the young grew restive in an environment that no longer appeared responsive to their needs. The reasons for the decline are complex. Everything from the widening economic opportunities for young men, which drew many of them away from the communities, to the change in the role of religion in American life have been suggested.

A community founded on a doctrine requiring the celibacy of its members in imitation of the life of Christ obviously cannot grow through natural increase. It must rely on admissions from the world. Its largest accretions have followed religious revivals, such as those of the New Light Baptists in New Lebanon, New York, in 1779; the Kentucky Revival in the early 1800s; and the Millerite excitement of the 1840s, when hundreds hearing the gospel of Christ's Second Appearing left the course of the world to enter the Society. Later in the nineteenth century, and through most of the twentieth century, there was little active missionary outreach, the leadership of the United Society primarily being concerned, perhaps understandably, with the care of an aging population, the maintenance and disposition of properties and the investment of funds. During this period, most Shaker communities, including that at Sabbathday Lake, came to rely for continuity on the children who were left in their care, expecting that many upon reaching adulthood would elect to remain with them; as the years passed, however, fewer and fewer stayed. By the turn of the century, the membership of almost all remaining Shaker societies was composed of sisters, many of whom were aged.

The fact of Shaker survival for over two hundred years must point to an essential strength in the church and its way of life, and many Believers have waited patiently for the day when a "new age of spirituality" would bring greater receptivity to its religious message. Writing in 1904, the gifted Eldress Anna White suggested confidentially that

[a]s mankind progresses in evolution toward pure spirituality, more and more will individuals find in advancing Shakerism, the physical, intellectual, social and spiritual necessities of being, met and satisifed.

Beginning with one or two individuals in the late 1950s, and accelerating in the 1970s, seekers, at first tentatively and later with greater boldness, have found their way to the Church. The possibility of a new generation of Shakers is no longer an academic question.

As we visit with the Sabbathday Lake Shakers through the four seasons of the year, a rich and varied way of life becomes apparent. Although it

Office woodshed in spring

draws from the wellspring of the Shaker tradition, it is not static. The little band of Believers in Maine may be strengthened in their resolve by the example of generations of saints who have gone before them, but they cannot rest on past accomplishment. It is the continual calling to re-dedication that lies at the heart of the Shaker way.

> The rolling deep may overturn, the valleys sink, the mountains burn.
> But thou my soul shall firmly stand, supported by God's righteous hand.
> To Thee O Lord my thanks I give, 'tis by Thy holy faith I live.
> My life I freely have laid down, to bear the cross and wear the crown.

I · WINTER

Do you hear the sounds of the winds that blow,
In the tempest wild across the snow?
They come in the shadow, they come in the storm,
That darkens the sky . . . with its awful form;
The bitter winds that find no rest,
On the sable cloud on the snow's white breast;
The bitter, bitter winds!

Yet winter hath joys our souls can sing,
'Till an echoing chorus angels bring.

"Winter Song" from *Shaker Music:*
Original Inspirational Hymns and
Songs (New York, 1884)

WINTER SETS IN EARLY IN MAINE, AND IT sets in to stay. The white blanket of snow that covers its pine forests and harbor villages seems to linger longer than in much of the rest of the country. If winter chills and blows define the way of life of down-easters, it also has helped carve out the conserving, practical, resolute nature that we have come to associate with Maine people. With their neighbors, the Sabbathday Lake Shakers know the winter. They have come to understand it and to accommodate their lives to its demands. In the old days, Shaker brethren, leading teams of oxen, were called upon each winter, often in subzero temperatures, to open roads lost under snowdrifts eight or ten feet in depth, sometimes working all day without food or drink. Stories of winter storms have been passed down by Believers through the generations, confirming the long-standing bond between them and an often harsh environment.

There was the winter of 1875, for example. One day in March, after the "most powerful snow-storm of the season set in," the sisters of the community were unable to return to the dwellinghouse from the village's shops, where they had been busy at their various trades. They were stranded by huge drifts of snow formed by especially high winds. The family journal records that not one sister was at the dinner table that day. The brethren, braving the elements, had to carry food to them. The next day, a group of brethren with four horses and eight oxen were out breaking roads through the drifts. Even at the end of that month, Sabbathday Lake was frozen three feet deep, allowing Brother William Dumont to cut ice in sufficient quantities to fill the Village icehouse not only for the use of the Shaker family, but for sale to the world. But this was not unusual. Brother Delmer Wilson, writing in his diary in 1887 as a boy of thirteen, records that the ice in the pond "began to break up" in early May, and that it was not until the sixteenth of the month that the blanket of snow standing behind the schoolhouse finally melted. And in 1892, Sister Ada Cummings in her "Notes about Home" for *The Manifesto*, the United Society's monthly publication, writes about a snowfall on May 21 that damaged young seedlings.

Winter in the Girls' Shop, 1901

We had frequent storms that winter and I remember one night, we didn't have snacks to pass around our rooms like nowadays. We waited till nine o'clock on a stormy night and no supper was brought over [from the dwellinghouse]. The brethren were very busy in the barns. At nine, Sister Ada [Cummings] told the girls to go to bed and the morning would come very soon, but they were crying as we got them ready. Then I looked out the window and saw Brother Delmer [Wilson] coming across the snow drifts from the dwelling house with a big pan of food for us. And we had a picnic. They went to bed very quietly and nicely.

Elizabeth Washburn

Settling Down

BUT IF THE Maine winter is long and harsh, it is a time in Shaker Village when both the hum of increased indoor activity and the hush of quiet sharing in prayer or reflection are perceptible through the long hallways of dwellinghouse and shops. Sister Aurelia had no dread of winter gloom. "What is that to us?," she wrote in 1883.

We but slightly feel its effects, hived together as we are in our pleasant dwellings, enjoying the hoarded increase of our broad fields, our gardens, orchards and vineyards.

For Sister Aurelia, winter was a time for "settling down" in cozy apartments. Sister R. Mildred Barker, currently the senior trustee of the Society, also draws a parallel with the beehive, but she likes to point out that Believers seem to re-

Brother Wayne on north porch, Central Brick Dwelling

verse the natural pattern. Winter is a time when members of the family busy themselves with the various trades that supply the gift shop for the summer season. Rather than storing their "honey" in the summer, the Shakers build up their store of supplies in the winter. As we will see later in this chapter, the sisters' trades have always been particularly active during winter. Sister Mildred has written of the close companionship shared by the sisters during the season

as we gather in the various sewing rooms, all nimble fingers improving the time that winter days afford by making aprons, holders and toys, or whatever we feel will interest the callers at the Gift Shop in the summer. We can here sew, chat, and drink tea, and the time flies all too quickly.

As the family gathers in peaceful communion during the long winter months, stories are shared, traditions are transmitted and songs are sung. As during the rest of the year, there are daily worship services, generally led by Brother Theodore Johnson. When large companies of children were the rule in Shaker villages, tales of other winters and of the exploits of Shaker boys and girls were told. One such story, that of the "little quail bird," so impressed Kate Douglas Wiggin, the author of *Rebecca of Sunnybrook Farm*, that she included it in her 1909 novel, *Susanna and Sue*, which was set at the Alfred, Maine, Shaker community, Sister Mildred's childhood home. (Kate Douglas Wiggin stayed with the Shakers at Alfred while completing the manuscript of *Susanna and Sue*. The wood-burning Shaker stove that heated her room in the Trustees' Office is on exhibit in the museum at Sabbathday Lake.)

The story recalls the missionary trip of Elder Calvin Green to western New York State in 1825 to gather a community of Believers there. Following an arduous trip and a full Sabbath of "la-

Sister Marie, Sister Mildred and Meg knitting

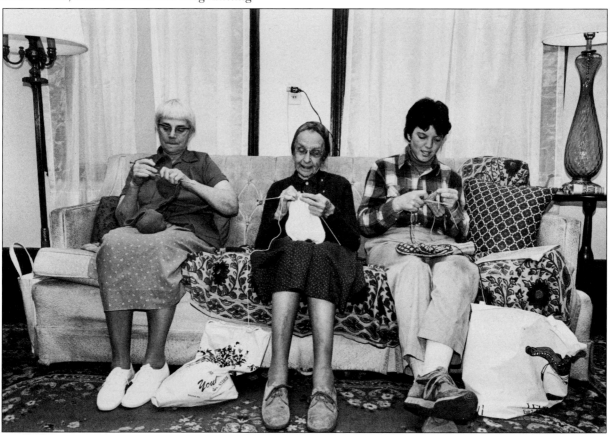

boring" with the local people, Elder Calvin went into the woods to pray. A young quail, despite its natural timidity, came up to him and he was able to embrace it, smoothing its feathers and holding it to himself. Nearby, a flock of adult quails stood, seemingly without fear, as if they approved Calvin's attention to the young bird. The elder saw this as a sign, as an answered prayer. He was not surprised later when a flock of quails alighted on the home of Joseph Pelham, with whom he was staying, "for the Shakers see more in signs than other people."

Just at night a young girl of twelve or thirteen knocked at the door and told Elder Calvin that she wanted to become a Shaker, and that her father and mother were willing.

"Here is the little quail!," cried the Elder, and indeed she was the first who flocked to the meetings and joined the new Community.

On their return to their old home across the state, the Elders took the little quail girl with them. It was November then, and the canals through which they traveled were clogged with ice. One night, having been ferried across the Mohawk River, they took their baggage and walked for miles before they could find shelter. Finally, when they were within three miles of their home, Elder Calvin shortened the way by going across the open fields through the snow, up and down the hills and through the gullies and over fences, till they reached the house at midnight, safe and sound, the brave little quail girl having trudged beside them the whole distance, carrying her tin pail.

The "little quail girl" was Polly Jane Reed, who was later to become a prominent Shaker leader, serving in the Church's central ministry at Mount Lebanon, New York.

Children have always been integrated into the fullness of Shaker family life, even when their numbers were sufficiently large for separate boys' and girls' orders, under the supervision of their own brother and sister caretakers, to have been the rule. Although frequently working side by side with the adult members of the community, children were encouraged to participate in a wide variety of diversions of their own that helped to dispel the gloom of the long season for young and old alike. The situation of the community at Sabbathday Lake, lying on the side of a long, gently sloping hill, still makes it ideal for sledding and coasting, a favorite winter pastime for Shaker children. The hill ends at the shore of Sabbathday Lake, where skating has always been a popular form of winter sport for Believers. Years ago, a team of horses hitched to a sleigh not only was a necessary method of transportation for members of the community, but also provided a fine means for an outing to see the splendors of the season.

Young Brother Delmer's diary seems to indicate, however, that for Shaker children, there was as much joy in the varied daily rounds of the community—in the faithful execution of responsibilities assigned to them and in the growing sense of their own increasing usefulness to the family—as there was their play. Delmer can write of setting up a swing in the barn and of having "some fun," or of taking the horse and snow plow to the pond for the sheer enjoyment of it, but a greater satisfaction seems to come from tending calves and lambs, tapping maple trees, assisting millworkers with their chores, hauling wood to the wash house or staves to the cooper's shop, and just experiencing the rather varied life of the community and the natural world around him.

Despite the tendency of some to see the Shakers as a dour, stolid folk, a surprising openness and true generosity of spirit mark their way of life. Even in the relative solitude of winter, a lively wholeness is evident in the Village. Indoor occupations are varied and there are ample opportunities for diversion. Today, it would not be surprising to find the members of the family sitting around a television set, much as families "in the world" do, but on other evenings the visit of friends might be the occasion for an old-fashioned Shaker singing meeting. In the earlier days of this century, and during much of the last, family entertainments were organized by the younger members, often with elaborate costumes and original musical scripts. Popcorn parties were another favorite amusement, everyone sharing in the production of this sweet, molasses-dipped confection.

Sister Marie in the quiet of winter, Shaker Village "back row"

The Yearly Fast

WINTER IS ALSO the season of several distinctive Shaker religious practices and observances that bring a solemnity to the season perhaps unmatched by any other time of the year. As we have seen, the practice of confession of sin is a fundamental principle of the Shaker faith. It precedes admittance into the church and is available whenever a Believer is burdened or troubled by personal failure or uncertainty. Brother Delmer liked to tell the story of Hewitt Chandler, one of the most resourceful and talented of nineteenth-century Believers at Sabbathday Lake, who is remembered for his hard work and inventiveness, although he did not live out his years as a Shaker.

Well, all through his growing up he had charge of the garden, the farm, the like of that. And Elder [William] Dumont told me that if he didn't do every stroke of work he should in the garden, that night he went and confessed it. He said, "I don't feel justified in my day's service."

Such is the nature of confession among the Shakers.

Very early in Shaker history, the practice of confession became associated with Christmas and the Christmas season. Father Joseph Meacham, who gave structure to much of Shaker life as it is still practiced, enjoined upon Believers in 1787 the duty of confession and reconciliation on Christmas, which he saw as the Shakers' day of atonement, consciously borrowing from the Hebrew practice. Later, it was ordained that this work be undertaken within the season of Advent, but before the day of Christmas itself, so that full reconciliation would characterize the holy day. From these beginnings developed the Shaker "Yearly Sacrifice" or "Fast Day," a late November or December Sunday especially appointed for the purpose of confession, contrition and repentance. Prior to the general "opening," when each Believer would confess to the elder or eldress, the family leaders themselves opened their minds to the ministry. Here is a description of the event, as it occurred in 1880, from entries in the official "New Gloucester Church Journal."

NOV. 27TH. SATURDAY A very comfortable day.

Eldress Hannah Davis and Sister Lizzie Haskell [the eldresses of the Poland Hill family] *came down from Poland Hill to see the ministry sisters this afternoon, to attend to the Gift of Confession.*

Church Elders have shared in a like preparation that they may be ready to commence the New Year, with renewed determination.

NOV. 28TH. SABBATH DAY. Our Yearly Fast is today.

The Elders and people of this place, as well as at Wisdom's Valley [Watervliet, New York] & Enfield, N. H. are this day, engaged in one and the same work, the confession of all past transgressions, in the Order of God.

May his blessing attend the gift. And the people be benefitted at the close of the day.

A general good gift prevails throughout. We have a very powerful meeting this evening. Elder John [Vance] and ministry sisters attend. Elder John has a beautiful gift in speaking, inviting us all to more love for each other, more devotedness to the gospel cause, and less selfishness . . .

Christmas

IF THE YEARLY FAST is a day for personal introspection and reconciliation, Shaker with Shaker, it is also a solemn prelude to the special joy of Christmas, anticipated with a growing sense of expectancy during the season of Advent in daily worship.

Shaker attitudes about Christmas may be traced back to the founder of the faith herself. It is one of many stories the Shakers love to retell. While still in England, there had been discussions among the members of the small group of Believers gathered around Mother Ann as to the proper day for the observance of Christmas. The issue centered on whether the church should accept the newer Gregorian reckoning of the date, or that of the Julian calendar. Later, in 1776,

Dwellinghouse at Christmas

after the Believers joined together in the wilderness of Niskayuna in upstate New York, Sister Hannah Hocknell arose early on the morning of December 25 for a regular day of household chores, but found that she was unable to put on her shoes. "Ever alert to spiritual signs in even the smallest occurrences in the 'daily round,'" Brother Theodore Johnson wrote in 1969,

Mother Ann quickly interpreted Hannah's predicament as an indication that the day was one specially set apart. She quoted the Lord's words to Moses on Sinai, saying, 'Put off they shoes from off they feet, for the place wherein thou standest is holy ground.' Mother saw, too, in Hannah's preparation for the cleaning of the Believers' temporal home, a sign that their calling for the day must be one set aside for the cleaning of their spiritual houses and garments. She appointed that henceforth the day would be kept among Believers for spiritual purposes alone.

In puritan New England, it may be recalled, Christmas was not observed until well into the nineteenth century. But for Shakers, ever since that first winter in Niskayuna, Christmas has been a special day. Its early association with the spiritual works of confession of sin and reconciliation, however, does not mean that eighteenth- and nineteenth-century Believers were unmindful of the simple joys of the day. This attitude is evident in an early Shaker Christmas hymn preserved at Sabbathday Lake. The first part of this 1807 hymn contains twenty-one verses, a length not unusual in Shaker music of the period. Three verses, perhaps, are sufficient to capture the Shaker sense of the day.

13. Brethren and sisters well agree
    And have our Christmas cheer.
    Rejoice in truth and equity,
    Because our Savior's here.

14. Oh, how his presence makes us smile
And doth our souls refresh
Each one believing they're a child
Of his forgiving grace.
15. Oh, come then let us forgive
That we may be forgiven.
This is the way for us to live
And be the heirs of Heaven.

It is the very essence of the Shaker way that the spiritual life of Believers and the practical daily rounds seem to be sewn together with invisible thread. Every act is infused with the motives of faith, and a division between the religious and secular is often difficult to find, seeming artificial at best.

As we have seen, the Era of Mother's Work (1838–ca. 1858) represented an especially intense period of Shaker spirituality, when the very heavens seemed to have opened to the communities. During this period, there appeared for devout Believers to be an actual and tangible blending of the physical world with that of the spiritual. It is not surprising, then, that the celebration of Christmas took on the deeply emotional, ecstatic characteristics of the times, when the spirits of saints and angels entered into the daily lives of the little villages. To outsiders passing through the Sabbathday Lake community in the winter of 1845, the neat buildings and lands of the community, dressed in seasonal white, must have appeared serene and quiet. But this was at the very height of Mother's Work, and within the Village a fire burned scarcely imaginable to the world's people. Intense physical "laboring" took the form of shaking and turning and speaking in unknown tongues. Messages from the spirit-land were received by especially gifted brethren and sisters known as "instruments" and transmitted by them to the other Believers. Through this medium, heavenly figures walked among the people, calling them to repentance, exhorting them to cleave more closely to the gospel way, drawing them into a more perfect union.

These visitations, a commonplace during the Era of Manifestations, were especially awe-inspiring that Christmas, and the messages were urgent and compelling. A description of the remarkable 1845 Christmas meeting has been preserved for us by Elder Otis Sawyer.

. . . the holy Saviour marched around, and spoke as follows, I have bro't you the bread, and water, of life eternal; present ye your cups and ye shall receive that refreshing water, and this bread of heaven.

. . .

Good Mother Ann again bestowed her love and blessing on all her faithful children.

. . .

We received some very refreshing love from the apostles; and showered our love upon each other, spoke our good faith and determination to persevere in the way of God.

Elder Brother then desired that we would all kneel down: and make 24 low bows in thanks for what we had received.

Add to this the almost innumerable exhortations to love, to zeal for the way of God, and the increasing work of the gospel; both from the old, and the young; from the visible and invisible.

These brief excerpts from Elder Otis's full account of that mid-nineteenth-century Christmas observance may give us a sense of the spirit that infused the Shaker communities during the Era of Mother's Work. For Shakers, a "lively," receptive spirit is a virtue to be sought after. Those familiar with the stately cadences of the church music of other denominations are often surprised by Sister Mildred's acceleration of lagging tempos in prayer services at Sabbathday Lake, calling the congregation to more "life." In Elder Otis's account of the Christmas meeting, we can almost feel this movement of the spirit as Sister instruments Rosanna Crowell and Sophia Mace, clothed in the dignity of the Savior and Mother Ann, play out their august roles among rows of Believers extending open-palmed hands to gather love, presenting cups invisible on the material plane to receive spiritual water and bread, and bowing and swaying to the strains of soulful prayer-songs, all drawn from the oldest traditions in Anglo-American folk hymnody.

Vestibule of the Central Brick Dwelling. The rockers are from the South Family chair factory, Mount Lebanon Shaker Village, New York (ca. 1900)

Well after the Era of Manifestations came to an end, inspiration continued to be a feature in Shaker meetings, if not as frequently in the day-to-day lives of Believers. In 1876, for example, the venerable Elder Joseph Brackett, (remembered not only as a saintly leader but also as the composer of "Simple Gifts," today's most widely known Shaker song) received inspiration from the Savior and was able to exhort the assembled Believers with his loving, inspired words. That was the first year the Sabbathday Lake Shakers had a Christmas tree, ablaze with the light of candles that "sent a thrill of delight mingled with love and joy through every heart." Setting the tone of many Shaker Christmas celebrations to come, the younger members of the family offered original compositions on the theme of the day and sang specially learned Christmas carols; a committee of sisters prepared wonderful seasonal decorations to enhance the festive spirit; and the seventy souls comprising the community of faith exchanged gifts, one with another.

Shaker children at Sabbathday Lake even began to expect visits from Santa Claus by the end of the nineteenth century. In 1896, the editors of the *Lewiston Journal* sent a circular to their readers, asking whether Santa Claus really existed. Sister Aurelia Mace, always ready for an intellectual challenge, took up the cause of Santa Claus.

To the Editors of the Lewiston Journal:

A copy of your Circular in regard to Santa Claus has been sent to me. I know not what may be the opinion of all Shakers, but our little ones generally expect Santa Claus to bring them some little present at Christmas.

Santa Claus really exists in the occult. He is the Spirit of the Yuletide Season.—Through his agents he at that time bestows many blessings upon the children. . . . I do not consider Santa Claus a myth. It is the Spirit of the Season. Therefore I would continue to teach the child to thank Santa Claus for filling its stockings from the beautiful rein-deer chariot. . . . We cannot take the mystery out of the child-life.

Today, the intensive but measured pace of life at Sabbathday Lake quickens at Christmas time.

Sisters and brethren alike will be busy packing tins of herbs and herbal teas to fill the holiday orders of customers throughout the country, while the cooks will be preparing Shaker boiled fruit cakes for holiday giving.

Traditional Holiday Boiled Fruit Cake

1 cup of sugar
1 cup of water
½ cup shortening
1 cup raisins
1 teaspoon cinnamon
½ teaspoon nutmeg
½ teaspoon cloves
1 egg
2 cups flour
1 teaspoon baking soda
Dash of salt
½ cup mixed fruit and nuts

Put the sugar, water, shortening, raisins, cinnamon, nutmeg and cloves on to boil at a slow simmer for 20 minutes. Remove from heat and let cool. When mixture is cool, stir in one beaten egg. Add 2 scant cups of flour and the baking soda with a dash of salt. Add the mixed fruit and nuts.

Pour into a greased pan and bake at 350 degrees for about 40 minutes. Be sure to test the cake, as fruit will make it soft in places and, if taken out before thoroughly done, it will settle and fall.

For the last several years, the pre-Christmas quiet of Shaker Village has been interrupted by the community's annual Christmas fair, which attracts hundreds of neighbors and friends seeking gifts unobtainable elsewhere. They come also for a variety of baked goods prepared by Sisters Frances, Marie and Minnie, and for confections from the capable hands of Sister Mildred, the community's senior candymaker. Herbal products, potpourri based on a nineteenth-century formula of Eldress Hester Ann Adams, and rosewater are popular items. Some visitors will seek a Christmas card imprinted with a motif from a Shaker gift drawing—perhaps printed at the Shaker Press—or an example of the Shakers' wonderful handicrafts. One also senses that many come for the special quality of Christmas sharing at Sabbathday Lake that helps brighten the long cold winter.

Christmas Eve brings the Shaker family together for Brother Theodore's yearly Swedish smorgasbord, a tradition of many years' standing. Over this attractive arrangement of holiday treats, the family meets in quiet, but joyful, communion—singing carols, laughing and sharing gifts around the Christmas tree, many of which are sent by friends in the world. Brother Delmer used to call this sharing of gifts "shaking the tree." In keeping with Shaker tradition, each Believer will have felt himself called to atonement, to a purging of self and self-interest. Coming at the end of a season of preparation, Christmas Eve allows members of the family to reaffirm their bonds to each other and to their faith.

On Christmas morning, promptly at 10:00, the Shaker family comes together for worship, joined perhaps by some close friends or relatives of the brethren and sisters staying with them for the holiday, and even two or three strangers from the world, drawn to Shaker Village for a sense of connection on the holy day. Even before 10:00, some members of the family and their guests quietly enter the lovely winter chapel of the Village's 1883 Central Brick Dwelling to sit in silent meditation before the sound of the bell at the hour marks the formal beginning of the service.

> As the Child of Bethlehem was to lead the lamb and the lion, so in this new dispensation it was the simple childlike spirit that must possess those who would hear and understand. Simplicity to Believers does not mean being weak in intellect, but rather undivided, free from duplicity, sincere and pure, as well as possessed of a childlike yearning to be taught.
>
> R. Mildred Barker

Everyone may participate in Shaker worship, and each member of the family brings a personal dimension to the Christmas meeting. Brother Theodore Johnson, the Society's current homilist, offers a message drawn from the biblical description of the first Christmas, but all may find a way of relating to the day. Sister Mildred, for example, may emphasize the virtue of simplicity, which she also characterizes as a "Christmas Gift," although of another kind.

A hearty Christmas meal closes the celebration of the holiday in Shaker Village, and a quiet winter repose sets in as the members of the family prepare for the New Year.

The New Year

THE REFLECTIVE NATURE of Christmas continues in the Shaker observance of the New Year holiday. None of the boisterousness that marks their neighbors' welcome to the New Year will be found among the Believers, but that does not mean that the Shaker New Year is a somber affair. To be sure, marking the passing of the years takes on a kind of poignancy in a Society no longer having great numbers. New Year's has always been the occasion for an annual recapitulation, when Shaker scribes and journalists traditionally mark off the gains and losses of the past year. But after years of diminishing numbers, where one by one "the ancients of the city" have passed away, the Society at Sabbathday Lake seems to be in a period of modest growth. A dozen or more seekers have "tried the life" in the last several years, including one married couple, and two—a young woman and a young man —are currently residing with the eight family members, and have "commenced to use the simple 'yea' and 'nay'" that characterizes the speech of Believers. So in the still, peaceful first hours of the Shaker New Year, there is much for which the little family still gathered in the way of Believers has to be thankful.

New Year's Greeting

Mount Lebanon, N.Y.

Listen! while we join with angels,
Who in love have gathered near,
And we'll tell you of the morning—
Of the glorious day that's dawning—
Of the new and coming year.

Clean shall be our future pages,
Stamped upon our mem'ry clear;
Free from sin, and void of sadness,
Fraught with joy and full of gladness,
Record of the coming year.

And we'll touch the muse, to waken
Those who are to us so dear;
Wishing all a happy morning;
Happy weeks and months are dawning,
And withal a happy year
    Shaker Music:
    Original Inspirational Hymns
    and Songs

Sister Mildred, one of the Maine Shakers' official diarists, has recorded her impressions of a recent New Year with her own characteristic sense of faith and simple wisdom.

The New Year crept in unceremoniously upon us. No bells or fanfare heralded its entrance for most of us had long ago learned that those who "watch the year out" never see it leave. Like the Shaker child who, seeing New Hampshire for the first time, said, 'Why, I don't see that it looks any different from Maine,' one sees no difference between the old and the new years that are but an instant apart. Yet we know that there is a difference, for one closes the door on the triumphs and defeats, the hopes and disappointments, and the joys and sorrows of the past twelve months, and the new year holds in its tiny hands opportunity, a forward look, a fresh beginning and new courage. So we go forward knowing that He who holds the universe in His hand and guides the planets in their course is not unmindful of His children and will supply "strength according to our needs."

Soon after New Year's Day, generally the first Sunday following the first of the year, Shakers listen to a reading of the Covenant, a lengthy instrument representing the community compact, the contract under which the Shaker com-

Shaker Church Covenant
Article II
Institution of the Church

SECTION 1. The object and design of Church relation:

We further acknowledge and declare that the great object, purpose and design of our uniting ourselves together as a church or body of people, in social and religious compact, is faithfully and honestly to occupy, improve and diffuse the various gifts and talents, both of a spiritual and temporal nature, with which Divine Wisdom has blest us, for the service of God, for the honor of the Gospel, and for the mutual protection, support, comfort and happiness of each other as brethren and sisters in the Gospel, and for such other pious and charitable purposes as the Gospel may require.

. . .

SECTION 4. Admission of new members:

As the door must be kept open for the admission of new members into the Church, when duly prepared, it is agreed that each and every person who shall at any time . . . be admitted into the Church as a member thereof, shall have a fair opportunity to obtain a full, clear and explicit understanding of the object and design of the Church covenant and of the obligations it enjoins upon the members. For this purpose, he or she shall, in the presence of two of the Deacons or acting Trustees of the Church, read, or hear the same distinctly read, so as to be able freely to acknowledge his or her full approbation and acceptance thereof, in all its parts . . .

Bread and teapot on old iron stove, kitchen, Central Brick Dwelling

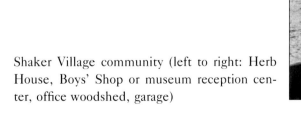

Shaker Village community (left to right: Herb House, Boys' Shop or museum reception center, office woodshed, garage)

munities are organized. In its current form, the Covenant dates back to 1830. This reaffirmation of purposes was once universally observed in the Shaker Society, but in this century, many communities discontinued the practice. It has been maintained without interruption only at Sabbathday Lake. Its provisions, representing an agreement between members and their leaders, cannot be amended unilaterally, and its yearly reading is therefore an important renewal of community values. The Covenant is also read when new members are admitted to the Society.

Important Birthdays

ANOTHER SPECIAL DAY for the Shakers occurs in February, the birthday of Mother Ann, the founder of the church. The actual date of Ann Lee's birth is lost in obscurity, although it is known that she was born in February 1736. From the early days, however, her birth has been celebrated on February 29, a day unique in the calendar. It is observed on that day in leap years, or otherwise on March 1. Throughout the years, major anniversaries in Shaker history are given recognition in daily worship; the births and deaths of a whole progression of faithful Believers are not forgotten. But Mother Ann's Day is a day of signal importance for the Sabbathday Lake Shakers. The Shakers of Maine have kept the older spirituals, hymns and prayer-songs alive in an unbroken tradition, and many of these honor the gifts, sacrifices and ministry of Ann Lee. While these songs are often used in Sunday worship throughout the year, they are a regular feature of the religious meeting on Mother Ann's Day. Here is a favorite of the Sabbathday Lake Shakers (See p. 67).

The song is believed to have been taught by inspiration at the Shaker community at Canterbury, New Hampshire, in 1849 by a mysterious figure called the Shepherdess, who visited several of the villages during the Era of Mother's Work.

A sweet tradition associated with the birthday of Mother Ann is the baking of a special cake that is served at the noon dinner on the day of the celebration. The recipe for "Mother Ann's Cake" varied slightly from community to community. One early version even required the rich batter to be beaten with sap-filled peach twigs clipped at the ends and bruised to impart a hint of a peach flavor. These days at Sabbathday Lake, Sister Frances Carr prepares the delicious cake according to an old Maine recipe.

Closely associated with the birthday of Ann Lee is that of James Whittaker, her successor as leader of the church. Father James was born on February 28, 1751, at Oldham, near Manchester in England. The Shakers remember him as a staunch Believer, unyielding in his faith, and often refer to his steadfastness in meeting. On his birthday, they frequently retell the traditional stories of his loving care for Mother Ann during the persecution of the church in England. According to the Shaker chronicles, Ann was imprisoned in the summer of 1770 "under a pretense of her having profaned the Sabbath," but it is very likely that these accounts refer to her jailing in the old Manchester House of Correction in 1773. Although the constable's records for July 28, 1773, set forth the expenses of "attending Ann Lees two whole nights," her confinement may have lasted two weeks or longer. Some historians have questioned the likelihood of the story that her cell was kept locked for two weeks so that she "could not straighten herself," and that the only sustenance provided her was a mixture of milk and wine fed through a pipe that was thrust into the keyhole of her cell by young James Whittaker. But contemporary accounts of the old jail seem to lend credence to the traditional story. Prisoners were not well treated in eighteenth-century England and relied on their families and friends for provisions or even the strangers from whom they begged food or alms from the windows of their cells. It is not unlikely that her devoted disciple stood by Ann during her imprisonment. His example continues to inspire the Shakers of Sabbathday Lake to this day.

I Love Mother

Transcription by Daniel W. Patterson

I love Mother, I love her way,
I love her Gospel precepts to obey.
The king may have his throne and the
miser his gold,
The monarch his palace and the princess
her home.
I covet none of theirs for I've the Gospel
call,
And a kind loving Mother, which is better
than them all.

In the Dwellinghouse

MUCH OF THE Society's life during the winter centers around the commodious Central Brick Dwelling in which all but three of the Shakers reside throughout the year. One of the sisters, Marie Burgess, moves to the large dwellinghouse during the winter, but makes her home in the Trustees' Office in warmer weather. As a means of conservation, the office and several other community buildings are closed for the winter months. Much about the dwellinghouse exemplifies the Shaker way of life. Its dual staircases, rising five stories from the ground floor, derive from the Shaker separation of the sexes. But their presence is symbolic of a community motive, rather than indicative of an artificial division among sisters and brethren. While it remains true that the north staircase is used by sisters and the south by brethren, the observance of separation has never inhibited the development of close and abiding relationships between Shaker men and women. Romantic or physical relationships, of course, are impossible within the context of celibate Shaker family life. Denial of the sex drive is part of the Believer's "daily cross," but even nineteenth-century observers commented upon the peculiarly sweet and affectionate regard in which sisters and brethren held each other. Shakers suggest that this relation between the sexes is freer and more open than wordly attachments because it is without the dominance of one over the other. In any event, it appears to have worked remarkably well throughout the history of the Society.

This is not to suggest, however, that there is not a sense of "order," between sisters and brethren, even today. Thus, men and women continue to sit separately during worship, enter the meetinghouse through separate doorways and eat at separate tables during dinner. But the presence of each sex, in its own order, complements the other. In 1793, Father Joseph Meacham established the custom of "union meetings" in which small groups of brethren and sisters met together regularly for an hour or so in the evening to converse or sing. This practice, instituted in Maine under the ministry of Father John Barnes, was intended to support the union between men and women in the family, and was informal in nature.

According to an old story, one of the Believers asked Father John what should be spoken about in union meeting. Father John replied, "Talk about anything. Talk about old Boney-part." The elder's reference to the emperor Napoleon may have been intended humor, but it points to the liberty granted to Believers in union meeting. Lest they become occasions for unseemly coquettishness, however, mid-nineteenth century rules prohibited the use of "fans, cologne water, or any kind of perfumery during union meetings," and required that conversation be "open and general," without "whispering or blinking." Union meetings were held about three times each week. After approximately seventy years, they were superseded by other forms of social gatherings. The Shakers are fond of quoting St. Paul that "neither is the man without the woman, neither the woman without the man, in the Lord" (1 Corinthians 11:11), and one senses this in every aspect of the Society's life.

Our societies are divided into families, varying in number from a very few to a hundred or more. These families consist of both sexes and all ages. Our organization, formulas and by-laws are anti-monastic. The sexes, however, occupy separate apartments (including those married, who have become members) all in the same dwelling; both sexes take meals in the same hall, but at separate tables.

Some people suppose that the opposite sexes among the Shakers never commune together; such are mistaken. While we live absolute virgin lives, there is much freedom in the social sense between the sexes, but it is required to be free from all that would tend to carnal affections and actions. The power thus to live in purity and innocence, is found in the conviction that a spotless, virgin, angelic life is the order of the Kingdom of Christ, and is higher, better, happier than a sensual, worldly life.

· · ·

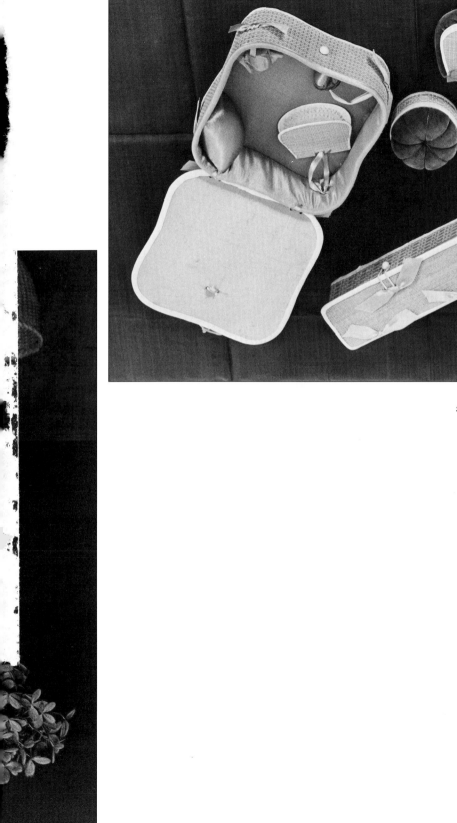

Woven poplar boxes, pin cushion, needle case
and Shaker silk scarf

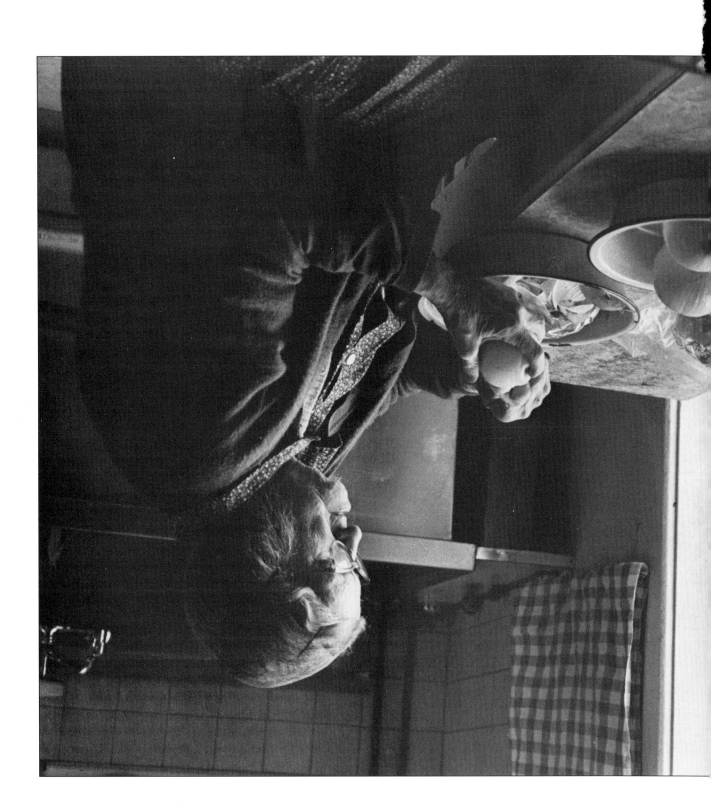

Small Shaker baskets

dollars to have a telephone installed that connected her "sleeping room" in the Trustees' Office with Eldress Lizzie's room in the dwellinghouse and with the family kitchen. But despite this inherent progressivism, "separation from the world" and the forces of tradition often have resulted in the maintenance of old-fashioned ways among the Shakers. New telephones now connect the various buildings of Shaker Village with the world, but Sister Aurelia's old crank-operated telephones continued to facilitate communication within the Village almost a hundred years after their installation.

This blending of the new and old in Shaker life is often a product of economic necessity or of a characteristic concern for the conservation of resources. Although several community buildings have long been furnished with oil-fired heating systems, including the Central Brick Dwelling, many rooms continue to be heated by distinctive Shaker wood-burning stoves that have provided over a century of service. The community at Sabbathday Lake did not found its own stoves but rather obtained them from the Shaker Societies at New Lebanon, New York; Canterbury, New Hampshire; and Shirley, Massachusetts. They continue to provide very efficient heating. In some rooms in the Village, radiators and stoves may even be seen side by side, offering alternate forms of heating in the same place. Wherever possible, wood, which is in abundant supply on the Society's lands, is used in preference to more expensive oil. Thus, winter sees the young brethren of the community regularly carrying wood from the Village's sheds to conveniently located storage boxes for use by all members of the family.

Woven Poplar and Other Winter Trades

FREED BY THE WINTER from most of the responsibilities of gardens and orchards (the apple trees in the Village orchard are pruned in January), the Shakers use the season to good advantage. The woven poplar industry has had an especially no-

table history at Sabbathday Lake. Indeed, the products of this trade, which eventually became staples of gift shops in several other Shaker communities, may well have originated in the Maine Society in 1869. A finished woven poplar box, lined with satin and decorated with matching ribbons, is as delicate as it is handsome. It is difficult to imagine the intense physical labor that went into its creation. But it is an effort well remembered by the many members of the Sabbathday Lake family today, although the production of woven poplar ended in the 1940s, and the boxes themselves were not assembled and sold after the early 1960s.

Sister Elsie A. McCool, who participated in the production of woven poplar, described the process in detail in an article in *The Shaker Quarterly*. Cut poplar from carefully chosen trees was carried to the Village's 1853 Great Mill, where it was sawed into twenty-four-inch lengths. The bark was then removed and the logs were split into eighths producing blocks two to two and one-half inches square. The blocks, which had to be kept frozen at all times, were trimmed to twenty-two inches in length and their tops chamfered. Then they were shaved or planed into paper-thin strips.

One side of the room in which the planes were located contained a long table set up temporarily for the processing of the shavings. Several sisters seated around it would straighten each piece of poplar by quickly drawing it between the index and middle fingers of the right hand. Care had to be taken to have all chamfered ends at the top and each strip laid right side down, as there was a right and a wrong side to each piece.

The strips were stacked into large baskets and taken from the sawmill to the laundry. It was still necessary to store them where they might be kept frozen. The next step in the process was the drying of the poplar. This was done in our large ironing room. The strips were spread around the room on large double racks on which the strips were repeatedly turned in the drying process. The intense heat of the room and the moisture from the frozen poplar soon produced a humidity which quickly exhausted the sisters engaged in the work. Several sisters worked in this department and had to

Meetinghouse and Ministry's Shop

The bell that calls the worshippers to meeting.

take great care that the strips dried flat and thoroughly.

After the strips were dried, they were gauged into strands one-eighth of an inch wide, a process that was accomplished by hand in the first years of the industry, and later on power-driven machinery devised by Brother Granville Merrill. These thin poplar strands were woven on special looms built by the Shaker brethren, containing a warp of 216 No. 30 sewing threads. The woven poplar, backed with paper and ironed until thoroughly dry, was then ready to be fashioned into as many as twenty-one different styles of boxes and baskets. Fitted to wooden bases, poplarware "fancy goods" included cases partitioned for jewelry and lined with velvet; sewing boxes containing emery-ball, beeswax, pincushion and needlebook, and a variety of other specialty items. Beginning in 1896, Sister Ada Cummings innovated by occasionally weaving strands of sweet grass with woven poplar for "ladies' work baskets."

Woven poplar boxes made at Sabbathday Lake were sold in the gift shops of other Shaker communities as well. In 1875, following a disastrous fire at Mount Lebanon, New York, the sisters of the Maine Society offered to contribute either poplar strips for weaving (or "webbing," as they called it) or unfinished goods to their Shaker friends in New York, despite difficulties in their own financial condition. The offer was gratefully accepted, and quantities of woven "popple," box frames, finished work boxes, and boxes for handkerchiefs, gloves, collars and jewelry were sent to the office sisters at Mount Lebanon so that they would not be without merchandise to sell.

A fine collection of woven poplar boxes, fitted with colorful satin linings and ribbons, has been preserved by the Sabbathday Lake Shakers, and it may be seen from time to time in special exhibitions in the museum at Shaker Village. Now avidly sought by collectors, they were once at the heart of the important Shaker fancy goods industry. They not only were sold in Shaker stores, but also were distributed by Shaker brethren and sisters on selling trips to guests in summer resorts throughout New England and along the Atlantic coast as far south as New Jersey. Today, they provide us with another example of what has been called the "consecrated ingenuity" of a remarkable people.

Of course the Society's industrial life in winter was not confined solely to the woven poplar trade. In former years, the Society's carding, grist- and sawmills were active throughout the winter season, and the Shakers maintained a vigorous business in the production and export to the West Indies of oak shooks for use in hogsheads or barrels for the molasses and sugar trades. Wooden pails, tubs and buckets of various sizes; churns; spinning and flax wheels; and sieves and dry measures were also produced, including a series of metric measures that were the first ever regularly manufactured in the United States.

Even before winter takes its leave of Shaker Village, the visits of a surprisingly large variety of birds serve as harbingers of spring. They are looked after tenderly during the cold season by several members of the family who take special delight in providing them with suet and seed. Chickadees, redpolls, woodpeckers, brown creepers and blue jays are winter visitors to Sabbathday Lake, and Canadian grosbeaks invade the orchard to the peril of young buds. A closeness to the natural world automatically comes with being a Shaker, one suspects. Sister Mildred has written of the simple joy shared by the family in seeing these little visitors. "Even amid the falling snowflakes," she wrote in 1969 in her "Home Notes from Sabbathday Lake, Maine," in *The Shaker Quarterly*, "they brought so much cheer and beauty to a cold and wintry world."

Not one sparrow is forgotten,
E'en the raven God will feed;
And the lily of the valley,
Heaven grants its every need.
Then shall I not trust Thee, Father,
In Thy mercy have a share?
And thro' faith and pray'r, my Mother,
Merit Thy protecting care?

II · SPRING

Our God whose wisdom made the earth,
Guides the rolling year,
Snowflakes, roses, red leaves falling,
And arbutus dear.
But among the types of beauty
That the seasons bring,
Best of all, the heart of childhood
Loves the gladsome spring.

"Springtime" from
Original Shaker Music
(New York, 1893)

IN THE MAINE COUNTRYSIDE, WINTER GIVES way to the warmth of spring only with great reluctance. Ice and snow may linger in Shaker Village as late as mid-May, and it profoundly affects the rhythms of life in the little community of Believers. But the Shakers know their land and its seasons well, and they begin to see signs of awakening life even in the midst of winter storms. Soon after the breaking of the ice on Sabbathday Lake, the strange calls of loons diving for fish, or of frogs "singing their tune," as young Delmer Wilson put it in his diary in 1887, are sure signs of the coming of a new season. The breaking of the ice also creates problems: spring is "mud season" in Maine, the water-soaked ground making outdoor work difficult and messy, at best. For the Shakers, spring is a time of expectant renewal not only in the pastures, meadows and woodlands that surround their village, but in their religious life as well. It is the season of Easter.

Lambs and Other Livestock

IT IS ALSO the time for new life among the Society's flock of lambs. In earlier years, the winter months, as well as the spring, saw the birth of calves. The Village cow barn, which was destroyed by lightning in 1951, was once home to a fine herd of registered Guernseys and some Jerseys, but since 1950, the community has not maintained livestock other than sheep. The lambs arrive in late winter or early spring, and they take the continual attention of the brethren of the family who are often required to hold vigils well into the night as the youngsters make their appearance. Just two or three years ago, the flock numbered as many as one hundred or more, but with the growing popularity of sheep-raising in New England, fewer numbers are currently maintained because they do not as readily find a market.

The loving way in which the Shakers care for the young lambs—the particularly helpless among the new members of the flock have even been taken into the Central Brick Dwelling during the first days of their infancy to be hand-nursed by members of the family—may be an example of simple human kindness, but it also points to the longstanding Shaker tradition of humane treatment for animals. In 1838, Nathan Williams, a member of the New Lebanon community, received an inspired message from Mother Ann respecting kindness to animals. In this vision, Mother Ann was seen stretching out her arms toward the animals and saying:

All the creatures that are gathered here in union . . . belong to the New Creation. They do not belong to the children of this world; they are under my care, and my eye is upon them and I know when they are abused and suffer cruelty. Poor dumb creatures were made for the use of man, and were put under his care and dependent upon his mercy and kindness.

. . .

You must have comfortable places for all the creatures you keep and see that they do not suffer in any way by cold, hunger or abuse. This gift . . . must go through every family of Believers.

Moses and Dmitri

Bright Monday Sister Marie discovered a lamb wandering in the fields. At first we thought the lamb had escaped from the barn but when a head count was taken, they were all found to be present. Evidently, while the family was at dinner, someone dropped this new born off intending that we bring him up.

Sister Mildred quickly named him Moses. Perhaps he was not found in the bullrushes, but he was found in the mud. As we had already completed lambing, it was decided to bring him down to the Dwellinghouse to live.

He quickly won our hearts as we watched him race all through the house with his almost constant companion, Dmitri [one of the family's pets, a bright-eyed German shepherd]. Dmitri had decided very early on that Moses needed that very special supervision that only he could give. They made quite a team as Moses would chase Dmitri out one door and Dmitri would chase Moses in through the other.

In the barn

In the nineteenth and early twentieth centuries, a curious public often took note of the proverbial Shaker kindness to animals. In the June 1910 issue of *Harper's Bazar,* a recent visitor to Sabbathday Lake reported that the Shakers "never abuse or speak a harsh word to their horses, which always look sleek." The writer found the Shaker treatment of chickens even more remarkable. They were so well housed and fed, she reported, "that their white feathers are always a degree more snowy than other fowls, and their yellow feet almost appear to have been polished."

Easter

IN THE SPIRITUAL LIFE of Shakers, the spring festival of Easter follows a period of Lenten introspection. Although the Shaker faith does not impose a fast upon its adherents during Lent, the weeks prior to Easter customarily are devoted to the study of biblical and devotional texts, and to the work of "spiritual housecleaning" at the same time that a thorough spring cleaning is occurring in Village dwellinghouses and shops. During the 1840s, at the height of Mother's Work, the Shakers observed a yearly ritual called the "Sweeping Gift." At a time appointed for general housecleaning, the community's inspired instruments marched among the Believers, sweeping "spiritual brooms" in symbolic movements and calling the brethren and sisters to inner renewal. Although the ritualism of the Era of Mother's Work is no longer a feature of Shaker religious practice, a song received by inspiration at Enfield, New Hampshire, in 1840, which is retained in the oral tradition at Sabbathday Lake, recalls the "Sweeping Gift." It may be heard regularly in worship services today (see above, right, for words).

In common with the Christians of other denominations, the Shakers observe Easter Week. A hallmark of Shakerism is the life-affirming nature of the faith, a fact that often comes as a surprise to those who perceive the celibate way of life of the Society as negative or denying. The Gospel lessons appointed to be read at worship services during the week reflect the mournful

Low, low, low, low in this pretty path
I will go,
For here Mother leads me
and I know it is right.
I will sweep as I go, I will sweep as I go,
For this Mother bids me
and it is my delight.
And a sword I will wield,
and a sword I will wield,
For Mother bids me so.
And I will hold, and I will hold,
For this is my work while here below.

events leading to Good Friday, but even in these there is an expectant emphasis on the Resurrection to be celebrated on Easter Sunday. While profoundly sensitive to the redeeming sacrifice of the cross, the Shakers do not dwell on the crucifixion and death of Christ in the dolorous meditations or litanies that characterize the Holy Week of other churches. Even among the thousands of Shaker hymns, anthems and prayer-songs, there are almost none that emphasize the Passion of Christ in descriptive detail. It may be that the joy anticipated in the Resurrection overshadows the earthly sufferings that preceded it.

In recent years, the Sabbathday Lake Shakers have printed special cards to be sent as Easter greetings to their friends. One such card, with words drawn from an old Shaker song, captures the spirit of the holy day for believers.

'Twas love that brought the Holy Lamb
Into this sinful world.
Tho' essence of the great I Am,
To sufferings he was hurled.
And now the resurrection light,
Like the returning of spring,
Fills true believers with delight,
And they Hosannas sing.
JOY IN THE RESURRECTION
The Sabbathday Lake Shakers

Sister Frances and Brother Wayne sharing thoughts

For the Shakers, Christ's overcoming of death at the first Easter anticipates a regeneration in which all men and women may share. Indeed, believers customarily call the Shaker way the "Resurrection Life."

The Shakers teach that the Resurrection Life cannot be attained without an inner or spiritual crucifixion, a process in which a man or woman dies to the "things of the world." A song from Mount Lebanon that was included in the Society's 1884 hymnal, *Shaker Music: Original Inspirational Hymns and Songs*, stresses this Easter theme. It is by Sister Martha J. Anderson.

Taking up one's cross and dying to the things of the world, the Shakers argue, is a freeing process, but one that requires self-discipline and daily effort. Among "Mother Lucy's Sayings," a compilation of brief texts and precepts collected soon after the death of Lucy Wright in 1821 and preserved in continuous use at Sabbathday Lake since then, are several that place emphasis on the cross.

Brethren and sisters, you hear a great deal about the cross; perhaps a great deal more than you want to hear, many times; but every one ought to consider that all they have gained toward the Kingdom of Heaven is by the daily cross; and all who do not carry the daily cross in all their thoughts, words and actions cannot travel far in the way of God.

Some think they have harder times than others; but such ought to consider whether there is not something in them which needs greater crosses to subdue, And don't you flounce or frown till you see whether you do not need all you have and more.

The spiritual quickening of Easter occurs at the very time that life quickens at Shaker Village. The arrival of spring imposes great and varied responsibilities on the members of the family. As snow and ice recede, vegetable and herb gardens must be prepared for planting later in the season; buildings that had been closed for the winter opened and cleaned; and the Shaker museum readied for the tourist season.

Resurrection

1. Dying daily 'tis the conscious
   Evolution of the soul,
   In a life of endless progress,
   As the ages onward roll.
   Dying, just as seasons changing,
   Leave the forms that pass away,
   Higher life, new growth unfolding,
   Smites the old with sure decay.

2. Dying to the loves of nature,
   Self and selfishness they hold,
   In a sphere too cramped and narrow,
   For the being to unfold.
   Dying, unto worldly honor,
   Glory's vainly boasted name,
   Laurel wreath of truth immortal,
   Never crowned the sons of fame.

3. Dying unto bitter envy,
   Jealousy and vain conceit,
   Demon spoilers, of the blessing,
   Shared where peace and union meet.
   Dying to life's sordid grasping,
   Love of power and earthly gain,
   That would rob a needy brother,
   Heeding not his want or pain.

4. Dying to a lofty spirit,
   Over-bearing, proud and high,
   Stooping not with gentle pity,
   When the lowly passeth by.
   Dying unto false pretenses,
   Held in pure Religion's name,
   Cant, hypocrisy and grandeur—
   Silken robes for sin and shame.

5. Dying, that in resurrection,
   Grand and true the soul may rise,
   Noble type of God-like image,
   Wrought through perfect sacrifice.
   Life is in the Christian's triumph,
   When from sin and bondage free,
   Lo, the prince of darkness cometh,
   And can find no place in me.

MT. LEBANON, N. Y.

1. Dy - ing dai - ly 'tis the con - scious Ev - o - lu - tion of the
2. Dy - ing to the loves of na - ture, Self and sel - fish - ness they
3. Dy - ing un - to bit - ter en - vy, Jeal - ous - y and vain con-

soul, In a life of end - less progress, As the a - ges on - ward roll.
hold, In a sphere, too cramped and narrow, For the be - ing to un - fold.
ceit, De - mon spoil - ers, of the blessing, Shared where peace and union meet.

Dy - ing, just as seasons chang - ing, Leave the forms that pass a-
Dy - ing, un - to world - ly hon - or, Glo - ry's vain - ly boast - ed
Dy - ing to life's sor - did grasp - ing, Love of power and earth - ly

way, Higher life, new growth unfolding, Smites the old with sure de - cay.
name, Laurel wreath of truth immor - tal, Never crowned the sons of fame.
gain, That would rob a needy brother, Heeding not his want or pain.

The Great Mill

FOR MANY YEARS, the early spring witnessed much activity in the Village sawmill, as most of the brethren and their hired men turned their attention to the community's extensive lumbering business. Occasionally, the operation was delayed by a lingering winter, when the huge pine logs were encased in the ice of the millpond, but the sawing of lumber was a regular activity during March and April at Sabbathday Lake from the Society's earliest days until well into the present century. As early as 1796, in one of their first communal enterprises, the Shakers built a sawmill just north of the Village, which served much of the surrounding area.

The people of New Gloucester and Poland took special pride in the importance of the local lumbering industry. With a touch of civic boastfulness, they claimed that the "best tract of pine timber ever known in Maine" was located between the Royal River and the Little Androscoggin. In 1853, the Great Mill was built, a structure sixty feet long and twenty-one feet wide. In the three stories and basement of this impressive building, the Shaker brethren practiced a variety of trades. In spring 1892, Sister Ada Cummings, the family's correspondent for the Shaker monthly publication, *The Manifesto*, reported that 254,000 feet of logs had been sawed at the Great Mill, of which 104,000 belonged to the Society and the remainder to its neighbors. It was here that the Shakers produced sieves and dry measures not only in conventional sizes, but in ten different sizes made in conformity to the metric system. Brother Granville Merrill made the molds and patterns for these measures in 1877, after which they were turned on a regular basis. According to the Society's records, these were the first metric measures ever regularly manufactured in the United States under license from the Metric Bureau in Boston.

The production of metric measures is another example of the Shakers' willingness to innovate and experiment in their industrial life. This characteristic progressivism is underscored by several other pursuits associated with the 1853 Great

Mill, as well. In one of the upper rooms of the Mill, the brethren manufactured the mowing or harvesting machine invented by the community's resourceful Brother Hewitt Chandler, in 1865. The "Maine Mower," for which Brother Hewitt received a United States patent, was sold to farmers throughout the state and elsewhere in New England; at the height of this industry, the Shakers built as many as one hundred for sale in a year. The invention reduced friction in the operation of the sickle by a novel arrangement of parts for the engagement of its gear. This resulted in a substantial reduction of draft. Advertising broadsides published by the community in the 1860s suggested that "for ease of draft, durability, perfection, and beauty of execution," the Maine Mower had never been surpassed. A testimonial from a farmer in Auburn, Maine, stated succinctly that the

Shaker Maine Mower that I used last hay season cut the grass as well as any machine I ever saw, and is a great favorite of the horses. *I can recommend it to any farmer that is in want of a mower.*

During 1872, the inventive Chandler contrived another machine to facilitate the work of the Society, this time in the manufacturing of oak shooks, one of the staples of the community's economy. For some years, the assembling of oak staves into shooks for use in hogsheads and barrels, many of which were intended for the West Indies in the sugar and molasses trades, had been an important industry at Sabbathday Lake. In 1872, for example, the year Brother Hewitt invented his device, over 300,000 oak staves were sawed during the spring season at the Great Mill. The device was installed in the Village cooper's shop, to which the brethren would haul the staves from the nearby Mill. This invention permitted the staves to be cut evenly, beveled, and assembled in a hoop with a minimum of labor. In 1873, Chandler improved the machine. According to the church journal, the device beveled, hollowed, bent and heated the shooks, and a long plane edged them with

one stroke, "leaving no handwork to be done, only to pack them." The production of oak shooks was a sufficiently demanding business in the last quarter of the nineteenth century for the Shakers to employ a dozen or more hired hands in their production during the season, in addition to the brethren assigned to the work.

Signs of Spring

ONE CLEAR SIGN of early spring at Shaker Village is the gathering of sap from the community's maple trees. Earlier in Shaker history, a special Sap House was located in the Village, where the Shakers produced great quantities of maple syrup and maple sugar. Frequently, the task of tapping the trees was assigned to the young boys. As a youngster in the 1880s, Brother Delmer Wilson, with this companion, Eddie Pierce, often attended to this chore.

In the spring we tapped two hundred trees and put up four hundred pails and Elder [William] Dumont and Eldress Lizzie Noyes they did the evaporation night and day sometimes for two, two or three days. And I've learned since that each gallon required about a barrel of sap and some of that was sold at a dollar a gallon.

Today, the Shakers produce and bottle a limited quantity of maple syrup each spring, but it is not an important factor in the Village economy. Customers at the Shaker Store snap up the few available bottles almost as soon as they reach the shelves of the shop.

Spring is a time for setting things in place after the ravages of winter. The righting or replacing of fences and resetting of stone walks is frequently a chore of the season. Occasionally, the weight of especially heavy snowfalls damages Village sheds and outbuildings. In March 1887, for example, young Delmer Wilson recorded the loss not only of a large shed in which staves for the oak shook business were stored, but the Village turkey shed as well. Both collapsed under the weight of snow and were complete losses.

Putting things in order may seem a predictable spring occupation, but it takes on a special significance for Believers. Soon after a stone walk was laid out between the Ministry's Shop and the gate across the road in late spring 1882, Elder Otis asked the brethren of the family to reset it. Because it was crooked, it offended his Shaker sensibilities. He reminded them that Father Joseph Meacham, who had established the "Order of Zion," taught that "all walks must be laid straight, fields laid out square and fences built straight." According to the church journal, the offending walk was taken up and laid out again, "which was commended by Believers and the world." Spring is often a time for renewing whitewash and painting Village buildings, too.

Planting Season

FOR THE BRETHREN of the family, May and June have always meant planting. In the nineteenth century, acre upon acre of rye, wheat and oats were sowed each spring, and large fields of potatoes, carrots, beets, parsnips, onions, celery, tomatoes, cucumbers, peas, spinach, cabbage, turnips, several varieties of corn, squash, beans and pumpkins were planted. Most of this was for home consumption, but produce was raised for sale as well. The Society also grew tens of thousands of vegetable plants and seedlings for sale. Tomato and celery plants raised by Brother Delmer Wilson in his greenhouse were sold in boxes to local markets in Gray, Dry Mills and New Gloucester, as well as in Lewiston and Auburn,

Meg with seedlings

for many years. In the period following the Civil War, the Society's gardener was Elder John Coffin. This consecrated Believer sold his plants, flowers and fruit over a wide area in an effort to raise funds for the building of a new dwelling-house. Although he died in 1870, thirteen years before ground was broken for the building, Elder John's early efforts helped the community realize its goal. Today, the family raises much of its own vegetables on the several acres that remain under cultivation, so that spring is no less busy for the young brethren than in earlier times.

Spring is fragrant with the scent of apple blossoms at Sabbathday Lake. The Shakers have maintained extensive orchards for many years, and new planting is frequently undertaken in May. In addition to the McIntoshes and Cortlands that have long been staples in Village orchards, such apples as Baldwins, Northern Spies, Astrachans, Winesaps, Ben Davises and even Winter Bananas, as well as pears, peaches, plums, and cherries, have been grown by the family's orchardists. In May 1873, for example, Brother Hewitt Chandler added one hundred Baldwin apple trees, one hundred pear trees and one hundred crab apples, as well as some currant bushes, to the already extensive orchards. Grapes and melons have been raised and strawberries too have been family favorites for many years; the sweet berries cultivated by the sisters in community gardens find their way into a wonderful assortment of preserves and pies.

Following the death of Brother Delmer Wilson in 1961, the Shakers were obliged to lease their orchards to an outsider. There was no one left in the community to oversee the operation. Until the anticipated growth in their ranks allows them to resume management of the orchard, they continue to take an active interest in the condition and productivity of its two thousand trees. Happily for anyone who has sampled Shaker apple pie, their lease provides that they may take as many apples from the orchard for their own consumption as they choose.

· · ·

The apple blossoms, though about ten days later than usual because of the cold, were as lovely as ever.

On a beautiful Sabbath afternoon, I walked between row after row viewing the loveliness. The warm sun was drawing forth their fragrance, while the air was so alive with the musical humming of the honey bees as they busily pollinated each blossom. My heart echoed the words of our venerable Elder Henry Green who, gazing upon this same orchard some thirty years ago when it was under the care of Brother Delmer Wilson, said, 'Eden was never lovelier.' All nature was praising God and peace was there.

Sister R. Mildred Barker
Spring 1966

The Seed and Herb Industries

THE PLANTING SEASON at Sabbathday Lake also includes two very important Village industries: the packaged garden seed and pharmaceutical herb businesses. Both of these were associated with the Shakers not only in Maine, but throughout most of their communities. The Shakers were among the first to raise seeds and package and offer them for sale in small paper packets. Previously, seeds were sold only in bulk. In fact, only one commercial firm in the seed business existed prior to the time the Shakers began their own seed industry, and that firm may have been influenced by its dealings with the Believers.

The Societies at New Lebanon and Watervliet began raising seeds in the 1790s. The account books of the Sabbathday Lake Society indicate that the first sale of garden seeds was in the fall of 1801. The first seedsman in the community was Brother James Holmes, whose father, Josiah, was among the first to receive the gospel of Christ's Second Appearing at Thompson's Pond Plantation in the early 1780s. By 1837, the business at New Gloucester and Alfred was sufficiently large for the two communities to be concerned about their respective patterns of distribution. Because it would be unseemly for Believers to compete with each other, the two Societies entered into a written agreement that divided the state of Maine between them accord-

Path to the apple orchard

Open farmland in the spring

ing to specific regions and routes. By the late 1870s, however, competition from commercial seed companies outside the state began to seriously affect the profitability of this enterprise, and it was curtailed. Elsewhere, at Mount Lebanon, New York, for example, the packaged seed industry continued to the last years of the nineteenth century and perhaps beyond.

At Sabbathday Lake, the first herbs raised for sale were grown in 1799. In 1824, the Society constructed an Herb House to facilitate the expanding business. It remains on the back row of Shaker Village today, the nation's only extant Shaker Herb House. According to the 1864 *Catalogue of Herbs, Roots, Barks, Powdered Articles, &c. Prepared in the United Society, New Gloucester, Maine,* published for Brother Charles Vining by a Portland printer, more than one hundred fifty medicinal herbs were offered for sale, as well as four varieties of culinary or sweet herbs packed in cannisters.

The pharmaceuticals were prepared in small, compressed cakes, packed four to a pound. They were also available for sale in bulk. Listed in the Society's *Catalogue* with their botanical names and properties in Latin, the varieties Brother Charles offered ranged from such common barks as ground poplar (*Populus tremuloides*), white oak (*Quercus alba*) and hemlock (*Pinus canadensis*) at twelve cents per pound, to royal cowparsnip (*Zizia aurea*) at a dollar and ten cents per pound. The Shakers purchased varieties that could not be gathered locally or grown in the Maine soil. Here is a sampling of the Shakers' herbal products in the same form as they were listed in the 1864 *Catalogue,* except that their curative properties have been translated from the Latin in accordance with the glossary the Shakers thoughtfully provided on page four of their publication (See p. 97).

In a footnote to his *Catalogue,* Brother Charles also offered "a choice variety of Grape Vines, Plants and Garden Seeds, of all kinds, raised for sale and furnished to order," horse radish in jars, apple sauce by the gallon or barrel, peach water and rose water, sieves and brooms.

A natural outgrowth of the pharmaceutical herb industry was a related business widely conducted in the Shaker communities, the production of patent medicines and other botanical compounds. Of course, the second half of the nineteenth century was the heyday for bottled elixirs and extracts, and packaged powders and pills of all kinds, in America. Their colorful labels and fanciful names promised cures of every malady, from the most dreaded and fearful of diseases to the comon cold. The Shakers, whose communities were long associated in the public consciousness with purity and wholesomeness, found a ready market for their products, many of which were produced from natural ingredients grown in their own "physic gardens."

Each community that participated in the production of medicine became known for specific remedies. At Canterbury, New Hampshire, Thomas Corbett was the physician brother for many years. His "Corbett's Shakers' Compound Syrup of Sarsaparilla," which was prepared "from roots, herbs and berries grown, selected and discovered by the Shakers," was advertised as "The Great Purifier of the Blood and other Fluids of the Body." Distributed at wholesale during the late nineteenth century by Weeks & Potter, the Canterbury Society's Boston agents, the compound was supposed to benefit cases of dropsy, scurvy, gout, rheumatism, "female weakness" and diseases of the kidneys, liver, bladder, skin and blood. In 1882, Weeks & Potter published *Mary Whitcher's Shaker House-Keeper* to promote sales of Corbett's Shakers' Sarsaparilla. The first printed Shaker cookbook, it contained advertisements and testimonials for the medicine alongside menus and recipes provided by Sister Mary.

A Perfect Health Restorer

For Dyspepsia, Indigestion, Pale, Thin and Watery Blood, Malaria and Liver Complaint, Weak Nerves, Lungs, Kidneys and Urinary Organs. Consumption, Emaciation, and Exhaustion of Delicate Females, Nursing Mothers, Sickly Children, and the Aged

CORBETT'S SARSAPARILLA
is simply wonderful.

Skeins of Shaker yarn

Nineteenth century Shaker dress with characteristic "cape" or yoke

NET PRICES PER POUND

Common Names	Per lb.	Botanical Names	Properties
Balm Gilead, buds	1 00	*Populus balsamifera*	Beneficial in diseases of the chest Unctuous, mitigating, healing Strengthening the stomach
Belladona leaves	0 65	*Atropa Belladona*	Relieving pain, stupefying, producing sleep Mitigating pain, quieting Acting on the kidneys, diuretic
Boneset	0 22	*Eupatorium perfoliatum*	Producing vomiting Producing sweat Permanently strengthening
Cherry bark, wild	0 18	*Cerasus serotina*	Expelling and allaying fever Astringent Permanently strengthening
Coltsfoot, root	0 28	*Tussilago Farfara*	Expectorant Beneficial in diseases of the chest Lubricating, softening, mollifying
Elm, slippery, bark	0 14	*Ulmus fulva*	Sheathing, causing warmth and moisture Diuretic Permanently strengthening
Fleabane	0 22	*Erigeron Cenadense*	Arresting bleeding Astringent Diuretic
Indigo root, wild	0 35	*Baptisia tinctoria*	Antiseptic Permanently strengthening
Life everlasting	0 18	*Gnaphalium polycephalum*	Strengthening the stomach Producing sweat
Maidenhair	0 28	*Adiantum pedatum*	Expelling worms Beneficial in diseases of the chest
Moccasin or Valerian	0 28	*Cypripedium acaule*	Permanently strengthening Strengthening the nerves
Poppy flowers	0 80	*Papaver somniferum*	Stimulant Narcotic Mitigating pain, quieting
Skunk cabbage root	0 28	*Symplocarpus foetidus*	Relaxing spasms, calming nervous irritation Caustic, having a hot, biting taste Strengthening the nerves

The Canterbury Shakers also produced "Corbett's Vegetable Family Pills," a laxative or cathartic "depending on the dose"; Corbett's Shakers' Compound of Wild Cherry Pectoral," a cough medicine; "Witch Hazel Tooth Ache Pellets"; and other remedies.

At Enfield, New Hampshire, Brother Samuel Brown developed the formula for "Brown's Shaker Fluid Extract of English Valerian," a medicine intended for diseases of the nervous system, palpitation of the heart, nervous headaches, hysterics, inflammatory diseases and burns. Under the management of Elder William Wilson, the production of "Brown's Extract" remained important to the very last years of the nineteenth century. The well-known pharmaceutical firm of McKesson & Robbins of New York acted as wholesale agents for the distribution of this product.

The Shaker Society with the largest patent medicine business was the community at Mount Lebanon, New York, where a long succession of skillful physician brothers and botanists developed an imposing array of popular remedies, many of which were marketed effectively for the Shakers by the New York firm of A. J. White. Among the medicines produced at Mount Lebanon were the Shaker Asthma Cure; "Seven Barks," a tincture of blue flag, butternut, stone root, goldenseal, sassafras, bloodroot and black cohosh; the Shaker Hair Restorer; Imperial Rose Balm; Mother Seigel's Curative Syrup or Shaker Extract of Roots; Shaker Digestive Cordial; Shaker Soothing Plasters; Shaker Family Pills; and Norwood's Tincture of Veratrum Viride, which was being sold as late as the 1930s.

A. J. White published many imaginative and well-illustrated pamphlets and brochures to promote the sale of the Shaker remedies in the 1880s and 1890s, including a series of colorful almanacs. These often contained amusing stories, facts drawn from Shaker history, children's games and, of course, advertisements for medicine. The advertisements emphasized the Shakers' understanding of the curative properties of herbs, roots and barks, and their skill in preparing effective remedies. To a public for whom the Believers were somewhat of a mystery, the advertisements occasionally suggested that the Shakers possessed a mystic sense of the order of things, too.

BECAUSE THEY SEE CLEARLY

By reason of their pure lives, the Shakers, some more than others, are able to read the hearts and minds of men more gross and sensual than themselves. This being so, why should they not also be able to understand the character of disease, and how to cure it better than those who have no insight into nature's mysteries? At all events it is certain that the power of Shaker Extract of Roots, or Seigel's Syrup, to cure where all other remedies are useless, shows the rare knowledge and skill of the people who prepare it.

A. J. White was not only a successful distributor of Shaker and other medicinal preparations, but also an accomplished herbalist in his own right. In 1881, he offered the Mount Lebanon Shakers the formula for a fruit compound laxative and asked them to produce it. Apparently the addition of a new product was beyond the capacity of the parent society, which was engaged very successfully in the large-scale production of medicines, and the Shakers there declined White's offer. They suggested, however, that the Believers at New Gloucester might be willing to undertake its production. The offer was accepted in Maine and the Tamar Fruit Compound, as it came to be called, was an important community enterprise for almost thirty years.

The production of herbs waned at Sabbathday Lake in the last years of the nineteenth century, although the Tamar Fruit Compound was turned out until 1911. To be sure, small quantities of culinary or sweet herbs continued to be grown, mostly for use in community kitchens, and lovage and sweet flag root were used in the preparation of the old-fashioned confections that still were to delight generations of Shakers and their friends. Here is Sister Ethel Peacock's recipe for candied sweet flag.

Advertising broadside for Tamar Laxative

Interior of the meetinghouse

In the 1960s and early 1970s, the herb industry experienced a remarkable rebirth at Sabbathday Lake as the result of the longstanding interest of Brother Theodore Johnson. Encouraged by the wide public attention herbs and herbal lore were receiving, Brother Ted converted a number of small Village culinary and ornamental herb lots into well-organized testing gardens. Before long, the Village store was offering quantities of sage, parsley, thyme, fennel seed, "Shaker fines herbes" and several other varieties in little blue-labeled jars.

By 1975, the reborn industry was ready for major expansion. Fortunately, a young brother, Steven Foster, had entered the family the previous year and was encouraged to direct his time and talents to the herb department. Under Brother Theodore's guidance, Steven planted his first gardens that year. Early in the spring, the ground of the greatly expanded gardens was ploughed and treated with wood ash, mulched hay, rock phosphate and hen dressing. That first season, Steven planted about forty varieties. Within two years the Society was producing, packaging and selling eighty kinds of herbal teas and culinary herbs, as well as herbal vinegars, rose water and a fragrant potpourri prepared from an 1858 recipe devised by Eldress Hester Ann Adams.

Public Meetings

WITH THE coming of warmer weather, the community again occupies all of its buildings. Those closed during the winter for purposes of economy are opened. Worship is conducted in the old meetinghouse instead of the winter chapel, and larger numbers from the world find their way to the Village to attend church with the Shakers. Through much of Shaker history, the Society drew a distinction between its public meetings and family worship. Believers welcomed outsiders to the meetinghouse only for designated services or at specified times of the year, generally the spring and summer; moreover, the principle of separation almost always required them to exclude the world from meeting rooms located within family dwellings. For a period during the Era of Mother's Work, public meetings were not held at all. Shaker worship, in its essentials, however, was no different whether the public was admitted or not, although the intimacy of family meeting may have been lost in the presence of large numbers of outsiders.

June 11, 1874. The day being remarkably pleasant, there was an uncommonly large attendance at our public meeting. Five hundred spectators or more were present. The house could not hold them all and it was surrounded on three sides by a gaping crowd at all the windows. It was a gifted meeting. Elder Nehemiah Trull delivered an able discourse from the text, "Ye do err not knowing the Scriptures nor the power of God." Meeting some over two hours long. Six brethren and two sisters spoke.

Church Record

A feature of public meetings was the presentation of a sermon by one of the Society's more capable preachers, on a prepared theme, intended as an introduction to Shaker religious thought. Among the prominent public preachers at Sabbathday Lake were two longtime members of the Maine ministry, Elders John Vance and Otis Sawyer; Elder Joseph Brackett of the ministry and later elder of the church at New Gloucester; and Elder Nehemiah Trull of the Poland Hill family. Elder Nehemiah's death on October 5, 1886, brought the long tradition of public meetings to a close in Maine. As in the case of the herb industry, however, the Shakers

revived the practice in the last third of the twentieth century. The only differences are that *all* meetings are now open to the public, whether they are held in the meetinghouse or family chapel, and the world's people tend to come as participants rather than spectators, because the dance in worship no longer is performed. (Occasionally, a special service, like the Rededication of the Central Brick Dwelling, is still planned for family members only.) When Sister Mildred and Brother Theodore enter the meeting at 10:00 A.M., members of the public are invariably sitting in silent meditation among the brethren and sisters. Some of them, in fact, have made attendance at Shaker Sunday Meeting a weekly practice.

The Museum

ABOVE THE WORSHIPPERS, on the two upper floors of the meetinghouse that once served as the residence of the ministry, are rooms that now form part of the Sabbathday Lake Shaker Museum. Established by Sister Ethel M. Peacock soon after her move to Sabbathday Lake from Alfred in 1931, the museum also occupies the 1839 Ministry's Shop, the 1850 Boys' Shop, and several rooms in the Laundry or Sisters' Shop.

The objective of the museum is the study, conservation and exhibition of the material heritage of the Shakers in the context of the history and faith of the church. While the collections of the museum are drawn primarily from the impressive examples of Shaker art, craft and industry preserved within the Society, the Sabbathday Lake Shakers also seek, through gift or purchase, to acquire additional objects related to their history. Occasionally, their continued search leads to important finds. In spring 1968, for example, the Society acquired an object associated with one of the first Believers at Sabbathday Lake. Sister Mildred reported its acquisition in her "Home Notes" column in *The Shaker Quarterly*.

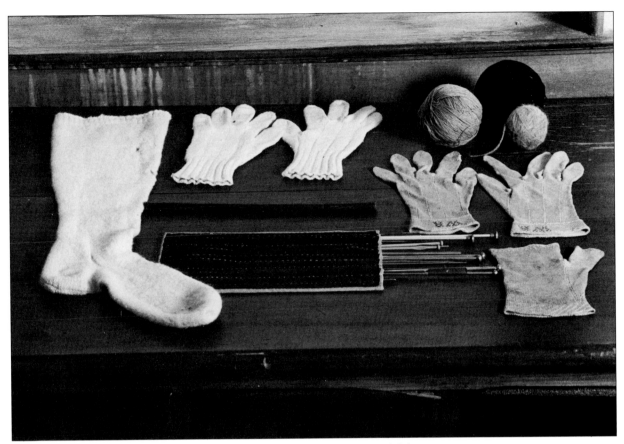

Nineteenth-century Shaker knit goods displayed in museum exhibit

A source of great delight to us is our latest acquisition to the museum in the form of a flax wheel made in 1796 by Elder Oliver Holmes who was the maker of flax wheels in New Gloucester, Maine. With the wheel came a letter of authentication written by Sister Aurelia Mace. She describes Elder Oliver as follows—"he was for many years the Elder of this society. Small in stature but great in intellect. A very good man. Eyes and hair jet black. His hair was always smooth and glossy. A beautiful singer and composer of music. Visited the Societies in different states in the year 1808 to teach them songs he had composed. He was twenty years old when he made the little flax wheel which belonged to Betty Nowell. She spun fine linen. Was also a tailoress. Lived and died with the Shakers. A very good woman."

Sister Ethel founded the Shaker Museum in 1931, but the practice of organizing exhibitions of Shaker arts and crafts for presentation to the world has even an earlier origin at Sabbathday Lake. On November 8, 1900, the *Lewiston Evening Journal* reported that Sister Aurelia Mace was preparing for an exhibit. "Just now Aurelia is getting together a collection of ancient articles," the report stated.

Mr. E. P. Ricker [the proprietor of the Poland Spring House] is to finish a room for the Shakers, either in the village or at the Springs, and in it are to be put all the quaint and old-fashioned bits of furnishings that can be found and secured.

Obviously intended for the interest and entertainment of Mr. Ricker's guests at the famous resort hotel, Sister Aurelia's efforts may have been the first attempt to display objects drawn from the Shaker heritage in a public exhibition.

Their museum is a source of pride to the Sabbathday Lake Shakers. Its collections include many fine examples of spare, elegant Shaker furniture, ingenious small crafts, woodenware and baskets, textiles, industrial arts and tools, and historic artifacts such as the saddle that Mother Sarah Kendall used when she traveled to Alfred from Harvard, Massachusetts in 1793 to take up her responsibilities as first eldress in the newly established bishopric of Maine. The museum is also important to the Shakers for the opportunity it offers them to tell their story to a growing public. Each year, it provides them with a modest income, a host of new friends, and an important resource for the development of new projects.

Woolens and Other Textiles

LATE SPRING IS sheep-shearing time at Sabbathday Lake. The medium long, fine grade of wool that the Society's flock of Cheviots and Southdown sheep yields is spun on several of the many wool wheels preserved by the Society, several of which are exhibited in the museum. Rural folk in Maine continued to spin wool on old-fashioned wheels until the very end of the nineteenth century, well after the traditional craft was abandoned in most of the country. The brethren at the 1853 Great Mill turned out sturdy but delicately wrought spinning wheels as late as the 1880s, and were still able to find a market for their product. Although spinning was not practiced at Shaker Village for many years, a friend of the Shakers now presents regular workshops there, teaching the intricacies of twisting and winding the wool fiber to members of the public. Skeins of Shaker yarn, hand-spun and naturally dyed in dark sheep gray, blue, green, rust heather, or other colors, sell well in the Shaker Store. The sisters also use this yarn to knit sweaters, mittens, and other items for sale.

Most Shaker communities raised sheep and produced wool in the nineteenth century. In some villages, flocks numbering fifteen hundred or more were maintained and spinning was a domestic art practiced by almost all Shaker sisters. As they worked at the large wheels, turning the yarn in graceful repetitive motions, the sisters often sang special spinning songs. At least one has survived in the oral tradition at Sabbathday Lake. Originally a work song, it is often sung in meeting today, the Shakers joining hands and gently stepping to its rhythms with swaying motions.

Round around our Mother's blessings,
Go round, round the world around.
Round around our Mother's blessings,
Go round, round the world around.

Twisting strands of love and union,
Into life's eternal blest.
Mother's hand is on the spindle,
Turning us to peace and rest.

Sister Tabitha Babbitt of the Harvard, Massachusetts, community was inspired by her work at a spinning wheel to contrive a more efficient manner to saw wood. Observing some brethren using a reciprocal saw, she noted that half the motion was wasted as the instrument was withdrawn. She fashioned a crude cutting surface around the edge of a tin disk, slipped it over the spindle of her wheel and tested the device on a shingle. It was a success, and Sister Tabitha is credited with the invention of the first American circular saw. The inventive mind of this talented Shaker woman seems always to have been active. She also devised a method of making cut (rather than wrought) nails, invented an improved, double head for spinning wheels, and at the time of her death in 1853 at the age of seventy-four, was experimenting with false teeth.

Before it is spun, woolen fleece must be washed or scoured and then carded. Carding is a process by which the wool fibers are straightened or aligned for spinning. Originally, hand cards (two flat pieces of board covered with leather and set with wire teeth) were used in the process, but in 1809, the Shakers built and installed a carding machine in the attic of their new grist-mill, one of the first carding machines in Maine. When the Great Mill was constructed in 1853, the carding machine was moved there and expanded in operation under Brother Ransom Gilman.

Wool Carding

For the convenience of Farmers and the Public in general, the undersigned hereby gives notice that he is prepared to card wool this season in the
SHAKERS' NEW MILL.
No expense has been spared to put the machinery in first rate order, and all persons having wool to card will find it in their interest to patronize the establishment.
RANSOM GILMAN.
Shaker Village, West Gloucester,
June 1856.

The old machinery continued to be used until late in the nineteenth century. Elder Otis Sawyer reported in 1874 that the "old ladies who spin" preferred the results obtained under the skillful hands of the Society's carder, Brother Josiah Noyes, over all others.

Another aspect of textile production long associated with the Shakers is weaving. (Indeed, Father James Whittaker himself was a weaver, and he found employment at this trade in Albany, New York, soon after the first Believers arrived in North America in 1774.) The Shaker Museum at Sabbathday Lake has several large nineteenth-century handlooms on display, as well as a number of specialized looms, all of which were constructed by the brethren of the community. One loom, for example, was used to weave the tape or listing customarily used in the seating of Shaker chairs, another for the weaving

of poplar "cloth" for boxes, baskets and other fancy work.

In a community that sought self-sufficiency, the production of cloth for a large variety of purposes—clothing, bedding, towels, personal accessories—was a vital function. The Shakers produced woolen, cotton, linen and silk goods (silkworms were raised at the Pleasant Hill, Kentucky, Society). Indeed, the leadership of the Society placed considerable emphasis on the establishment and maintenance of textile production within the communities. Although hand-woven cloth was not generally produced in Shaker communities after the late nineteenth or very early twentieth centuries, Believers engaged in rug weaving until the 1940s. In the early 1970s, Sister Elsie A. McCool, then over seventy years of age, returned to the looms to weave small carpets and table runners for sale in the Village shop. Her work demonstrated the perfection long associated with Shaker weavers.

Sister Elsie, a distinguished needlewoman, is the last of the Shaker cloak makers. Sometime late in the nineteenth century, Shaker sisters in several communities began producing a version of the cloak or cape that had long been a feature of Believers' dress, for sale to the world. The elegant Shaker cloak became a fashionable item of evening attire, with its lovely silk lining, attached hood and long silk ribbons tied at the chin.

The Shakers like to recount how Mrs. Grover Cleveland ordered a Shaker cloak in gray from the Mount Lebanon Shakers to wear to her husband's inauguration in 1892. After finishing the garment, the sisters discovered a flaw that only they could see. They immediately set the first cloak aside and made another one, their Shaker sensibilities having been offended by this little breach in the structure of perfection in which they attempted to live and work.

The longest tradition in Shaker cloak making has been at Sabbathday Lake, where Eldress Elizabeth Noyes directed the work. A wonderful early-twentieth-century example from the hands of Sister Sarah Fletcher is on exhibition at the Sabbathday Lake Shaker Museum. The sisters continued to produce cloaks regularly until the

Sister Mildred at one of several community looms

Raw wool and swift or skein winder

Loom and carding implements

Hand cards and wool

1940s. Since then, special orders have been filled by Sister Elsie from time to time.

As the members of the Sabbathday Lake community prepare the museum for the busy summer season, weed and hoe the gardens, and continue in the paths of work and worship, they are aware of the special loveliness of spring in Shaker Village. The Maine Shakers have always had a fondness for June, despite the arrival of black flies in numbers "thick enough to choke an elephant," as Brother Delmer used to put it. Sister Aurelia, surveying her home in June 1883, was moved to write a letter to the editors of the *Bangor Messenger*. Describing the month as the loveliest time of the year, with its blooming lilacs and apple blossoms and the deep green foliage of rows of shade trees, she exclaimed

Vineyards, gardens, orchards, and cultivated fields all around us in whatever direction we turn our eyes, and in our hearts that peace which passeth understanding. Surely the Utopia of Sir Thomas More is outdone. . . .

"*Come and see,*" *she wrote,* "*for we want you to know.*"

III · SUMMER

Light, light is shining all over Zion!
Oh! let us bask in its rays from above;
'Tis the lovingkindness of the Omnipotent;
'Tis but a proof of an Infinite Love.

Smile on us, Father, thro' the clear sunlight,
When tears of affliction mingle with our joys;
Bless us Heav'nly Mother, from Thy throne of mercy,
Till we're perfected for Thy lasting choice.

"Light, Light Is Shining." from *Shaker Music:*
Original Inspirational Hymns and Songs
(New York, 1884)

SUMMER IS A TIME OF FULLNESS AT Sabbathday Lake. The white buildings of Shaker Village seem to glow in the warm sunlight, almost like so many jewels set out in green fields and abundant gardens. The long, bright days of the season beckon to summer visitors. They arrive in great numbers in cars and vans and campers to see the museum and tour the grounds of the community. If their presence interrupts the tranquillity of Shaker Village, it is a disturbance the Believers accept with characteristic patience and good humor. As a major source of revenue for the Sabbathday Lake Shakers, tourism is encouraged. In addition, at least some of those who come as casual visitors are drawn to the life and witness of the Believers and return as friends.

The Summer Family

THE PRESENCE OF large numbers of outsiders in the Village sets summer apart from the rest of the year. Indeed, it is the overriding fact of the season. To help the Shakers cope with this annual invasion of their home, an expanded "summer family" joins the community each year, substantially increasing its ranks.

Ruth Perkins Nutter was raised by the Shakers at Alfred, Maine, and lived there as a Believer for much of the earlier part of her life. About ten years ago, Sister Eleanor Philbrook invited her to return to assist in the Shaker Store. She has come each summer since then and, when needed, during the rest of the year, too, patiently answering the sometimes impertinent questions of tourists, and helping them to select a purchase from the fine wares on display.

Others too, from teenage tour guides to senior citizens who help in the community's fields and gardens, return year after year. The presence of this enlarged family affords a sense of the Village as it must have been thirty, forty or more years ago. Twenty-five or even more at the dinner table is not unusual during the summer. Summer life at Sabbathday Lake is full and animated. But even with all the visitors coming and going, the sure rhythms of family life remain. The ordered

routines of work and worship continue without significant change.

Although the presence of considerable numbers of outsiders is primarily a feature of summer life in the Village, non-Shakers were once well integrated with the economic life of the Society throughout the entire year. As we have seen, self-sufficiency has been an important goal for Believers ever since the earliest establishment of their communities in Gospel Order, but it is an objective that has never been fully attained. Hired laborers have been necessary to supplement the efforts of the brethren, especially in large-scale industrial pursuits, even when greater numbers filled their ranks. At Sabbathday Lake, resident non-Believers lived in the Hired Men's Shop, which was located just south of the Trustees' Office. In 1875, the Shakers built another boardinghouse for their laborers immediately adjacent to the Great Mill, where many of them were employed. It was the obligation of the office sisters, for whom the conduct of business with the world and the reception of visitors were principal responsibilities, to prepare meals for the hired men. A commodious kitchen for this purpose is located in the basement of the office, although it is no longer in use. Separate lodging and meals assured at least a degree of distance between Believers and "the element of the world," but the Shakers and their workers often developed bonds of mutual respect and, occasionally, of friendship.

Hired men often had more than a little curiosity about their employers and came to know them well. "You could work a hundred years among them Shakers," Wendell May, a former hired man recalled,

and you'd never hear a word about their work or about any of their neighbors around. They're closed-mouthed. They've got a religion and they live by it.

I'll say one word for him [Brother Delmer Wilson, May's employer]: he was the nicest singer you ever heard. A voice like a lion and he sang bass. I used to go up in the back of the hen yard, lay down on the grass and hear Delmer preach and sing songs [from the family chapel, which overlooks the field from which

Sister Marie Burgess in Shaker Store, Trustee's Office

Shaker basket

Sister Minnie with young visitor

May would listen to Shaker meeting]. He was a good speaker.

Occasionally, hired men have been moved sufficiently by their exposure to life in the community to leave the ways of the world and to make their profession as Shakers. Granville Merrill began working for the community in 1858 at the age of nineteen. After ten years of service, he opened his mind to the novitiate elder, Alonzo Gilman, and entered community life. In the ten years he lived as a Shaker before his death at the age of thirty-nine in 1878, Brother Granville was one of the most resourceful and inventive of nineteenth-century Believers.

Several stories about hired men at Poland Hill have been preserved, especially in connection with the construction of the family's great granite dwellinghouse, which was not completed for many years. One day an aged man came to the Shakers and asked to be employed in finishing the interior of the structure. The Believers hired him and found him to be "very quiet, and as peaceable and as prudent as a man can be." They also admired the quality of his workmanship. During the spring of 1877, Eldresses Hester Ann Adams and Mary Ann Gillespie visited the dwelling to see how the old man was getting along.

While there, he asked them if they ever knew how he offered to take the job. They answered *Nay.* He then said,

That *little woman (meaning his wife) with whom I once lived, was much interested in this house. She seemed to be much burdened at times, and would often say what a pity that building cannot be finished up. Well, after she passed away that burden rested upon me, and I could not throw it off. It followed me until I had made up my mind to offer to take the job. Then I felt released.*

He further added, "I am a man of years, and it is undoubtedly my last work on earth. I hope to see it completed."

A late-nineteenth-century account of another hired man at Poland Hill, however, tells a different kind of story. It is included here, as published in an 1890 history of the town of Poland, because it provides a sense of the irreverent but kindly way their neighbors often perceived the Shakers.

A man of the world, as they called him, was once employed to repair their clocks, of which they had a large number. The Elder, [Nehemiah] Trull, finding him a good workman, and clear-headed, importuned him to join the family.

"Why," replied the man of sin, as he was denominated, "what in the world do you want of me who am unable to do farm work?"

"Ah!" said the elder, "we have help enough, but lack brains to manage."

"I dare say," replied the man of sin, "those who have brains are sure to run away; now I have a wife and a child who are all the world to me, and never leave my mind while absent; without them my life would be a blank."

"There, there," exclaimed the elder, "you are a man of sin and you must get out of that, or be lost." This led to a furious contest in which the Shakers were worsted.

"Why, I do believe," chimed in an ancient dame, "that a man who has a virtuous loving wife, and an intelligent and promising family of children, is to be envied."

"Prudence," roared the now infuriated elder, an angry frown upon his brow, "you should have a different name."

The Fourth of July

SUMMER IS A season of celebrations at Shaker Village. The first of these, of course, is the Fourth of July, which the Shakers observe with the same festive spirit as their fellow citizens. Independence Day in the country generally means picnics and cookouts; Shaker Village is no exception to the rule. The holiday often finds the members of the expanded summer family gathered around a barbecue on the lawns of the community, enjoying good fellowship and food. Some may even attend a nearby fireworks display. The celebration of America's nationhood in a Shaker community may strike some observers as ironic. After all, in keeping with the doctrine of separation, the Shakers do not vote or take part in political affairs. Furthermore, as noncombatants, they do not serve in the armed forces. The fact is that the Shakers do celebrate America, and they have been doing so joyously ever since Father James Whittaker received his vision of the new land on the road to Manchester in 1773. "When we were in England . . . ," he recalled later in his life,

some of us had to go twenty miles to meetings; and we travelled nights on account of persecution. One saturday night, while on our journey, we sat down by the side of the road to eat some victuals. While sitting there, I saw a vision of America, and I saw a large tree, and every leaf thereof shown with such brightness, as made it appear like a burning torch, representing the Church of Christ which will yet be established in this land.

James's vision was confirmed by several of his companions on that evening journey many years ago; "some could hardly wait for the others to tell them their gift; and we had a joyful meeting, and danced till morning." As it had for many others seeking freedom of conscience, America was to provide a secure home for the Believers, and their celebration of the nation's independence is an expression of gratitude for the many gifts the church has received in this free land.

At the same time, it is clear that the principle of separation occasionally resulted in tensions between Believers and the civil authorities, especially in the early years of the Society's history here. During the American Revolution, the practice of pacifism among the Shakers caused them to be viewed as British sympathizers, or worse, as spies for the Crown. Mother Ann herself was imprisoned briefly in Poughkeepsie, New York,

Rights of Conscience

Text: *Millennial Praises*, pp. 281–285.

Transcription by Daniel W. Patterson

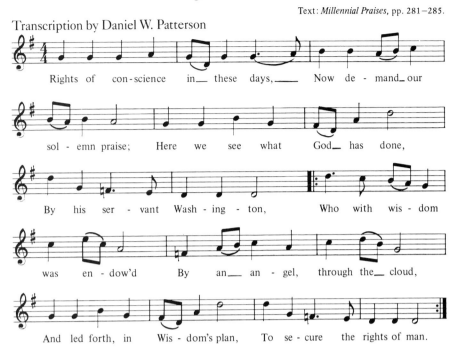

Rights of con-science in these days, Now de - mand our sol - emn praise; Here we see what God has done, By his ser - vant Wash - ing - ton, Who with wis - dom was en - dow'd By an an - gel, through the cloud, And led forth, in Wis - dom's plan, To se - cure the rights of man.

1. Rights of conscience in these days,
   Now demand our solemn praise;
   Here we see what God has done,
   By his servant Washington,
   Who with wisdom was endow'd
   By an angel, through the cloud,
   And led forth, in Wisdom's plan,
   To secure the rights of man.

2. "Arm yourselves, unsheath the sword!
   (Cries this servant of the Lord,)
   Rights of freedom we'll maintain,
   And our independence gain."
   Fleets and armies he withstood,
   In the strength of Jehu's God;
   Proud Cornwallis and Burgoyne,
   With their armies soon resign.

3. Thus the valiant conqu'ror stood
   To defend his country's good,
   Till a treaty he confirms,
   Settling peace on his own terms.
   Having clos'd these warlike scenes,
   Chosen men he then convenes;
   These a constitution plan'd,
   To protect this ransom'd land.

4. Prince of all the host he stands,
   Keeps the helm in his own hands,
   Till a law stands to declare,
   Bind the conscience if you dare!
   Then he spreads the eagle's wings
   (Signs of freedom) on all things,
   Form'd an order to his mind,
   Blest the earth and then resign'd.

5. When by precept he had shown
   What kind heaven had made known,
   By example aids the cause,
   Forms his own domestic laws,
   Breaks the yoke at his own door,
   Clothes the naked, feeds the poor,
   Bondage from his house he hurl'd,
   Freed his slaves and left the world.

6. Cyrus-like, was Washington
   Call'd to do what he has done;
   We his noble acts record,
   Tho' he did not know the Lord:
   As a prudent man of blood,
   He the hosts of earth withstood;
   Nature's rights he did restore,
   God from him requir'd no more.

Homemade breads and pie for the family's
Fourth of July picnic

Mixing bowls

and several Believers were summoned before New York's Commission for Detecting and Defeating Conspiracies in 1778–1780 on charges that they refused to take up arms and were persuading their countrymen to do the same. In the end, the Shakers either were vindicated or released as deluded but harmless, perhaps "infatuated" by their faith. Despite these unhappy confrontations during the Revolution, the Shakers viewed American separation from Great Britain as part of the divine purpose. Indeed, Elder Issachar Bates, who had served in the colonial militia from 1775–80 before he became a Believer, composed a hymn to celebrate the American victory. It was included in *Millennial Praises*, the Society's first printed hymn book, in 1812 and 1813. (See p. 115).

Although there would be occasional confrontations between the Shakers and the civil and military authorities until the period following the Civil War, it is a credit to the spirit of American democracy that Believers' "rights of conscience" generally were respected after the Revolution. The legislature of the Commonwealth of Massachusetts, which until 1820 included the District of Maine, heard a petition seeking the exemption of Shakers from military service as early as 1788.

In 1792, Amos Buttrick, a member of the Shaker community at Shirley, Massachusetts, petitioned the legislature to rescind his military pension on conscientious grounds. It was the Shaker view, as first enunciated by Father Joseph Meacham, that Believers should refuse all forms of payment for prior military service if their witness for peace was to be consistent and true. Before entering the Society under the ministration of Mother Ann, Buttrick had served in the Massachusetts militia during the Revolution and was injured in 1776 at the Battle of White Plains. Faced with this unprecedented request, the legislature passed a resolution granting the petition and allowing Buttrick to return more than eighty-two pounds to the state, as well as canceling all further payments to him. It was later estimated that the New Gloucester Shakers alone would have been entitled to receive almost $90,000 in accrued military pensions if the eligi-

Sister Mildred at front entrance of central Brick
Dwelling

ble brethren among them exercised their rights under the law.

In 1809, Massachusetts resolved the issue for Believers in the Commonwealth by enacting a law that exempted them from military duty, a principle that would be retained in the constitution of the new state of Maine when it separated from Massachusetts and became the twenty-third state in 1820. The exemption clause was the subject of considerable debate in the proceedings of the constitutional convention held in Portland in October 1819. John Holmes, then a member of Congress from Maine and later a United States Senator, spoke eloquently for the proposition. A resident of the town of Alfred, Holmes was a leader in the movement for separation from Massachusetts. He was to have a long and important career in the public service of the state and may be counted among those eminent American men of affairs—like Martin Van Buren of New York and Franklin Pierce of New Hampshire—who placed themselves at the disposal of Believers in courtrooms and legislative halls. (Interestingly, one of his first cases as a young lawyer was *against* the Alfred Shakers, a suit brought by Margaret Philpot to recover a bed "left among them.") Standing before the assembled delegates, Holmes asserted that the Shakers were entitled to the exemption.

This singular people contribute nothing to the increase of mankind and very properly refuse to aid in their destruction. They are not of the world; they are not made of flesh and blood. They share none of the extravagances of society, and wish to be exempted from the effect of them.

The proposition carried:

Article VII. Section 5. Persons of the denomination of Quakers and Shakers, Justices of the Supreme Judicial Court and Ministers of the Gospel may be exempted from military duty, but no other person of the age of eighteen and under the age of forty-five years, excepting officers of the militia, who have been honorably discharged, shall be so exempted, unless he shall pay an equivalent to be fixed by law.

Because voting would introduce a partisan element into the life of a community that seeks union in all things, the Shakers do not vote. It is also feared that participation of politics might draw Believers too deeply into the ways of the world. Occasionally, however, some communities have relaxed this rule for local elections or referendums, where issues having a direct impact on the Shakers were involved, or even for national contests. In November 1928, *The New York Times* reported that the Mount Lebanon Shakers were planning to vote for the first time in many years. The Sabbathday Lake Shakers did not follow suit.

MAINE SHAKERS SHUN VOTE.

New Gloucester Colony not to follow New York Group, member said.

New Gloucester, Me. Nov. 3. While the Shaker Colony at Mount Lebanon, N.Y. is reported as planning to vote Tuesday for the first time in 52 years, Maine's Shaker settlement here has "something else to do on election day."

Informed that the New York Shakers were said to be fully registered for the first time since the Tilden-Hayes campaign, a Shaker sister here declared, "I don't believe that is true. At any rate we are not going to vote here. We have something else to do on election day."

The fact that the Shakers celebrate the Fourth of July as all Americans do, although they neither bear arms nor participate in partisan politics, should not be viewed as inconsistent. Throughout their history, Believers have demonstrated a profound concern for the welfare of their country and, indeed, the world. They have responded generously in cases of need outside their communities; have expressed their views publicly on a wide variety of issues confronting the nation, especially women's rights and peace; and customarily have included the needs of their country and its citizens in their prayers. The North Family of Mount Lebanon convened a peace conference at the New York village on August 31, 1906, which many of the day's leading advocates for international disarmament attended. Eldress Anna White, then seventy-five years of age, addressed the hundreds of men and women who assembled in the meetinghouse that afternoon. Speaking on behalf of all Shakers, she said,

[Y]ou may think that, cloistered as we are from the outside world, pursuing the even tenor of our ways, the larger affairs of life, those pertaining to country and nation and not directly affecting us, would not enlist our sympathy nor engage our attention. It is far otherwise. No citizen is more thoroughly alive to the interests of the state or nation than are the Shakers. In the Peace of the nation is our Peace. The cause of Peace is our cause; its friends are our friends, and the opponents of Universal Peace . . . are our particular friends, for they, above all others, stand in need of friends.

In November 1906, the formidable Eldress Anna carried the resolutions adopted at the Shaker Peace Conference to Washington, D.C., where in a personal interview with President Roosevelt, she conveyed her own concerns, and those of her people, to the nation's leader. Although more conservative Shakers resisted the activism of the North Family at Mount Lebanon, the movement as a whole has concerned itself with all forms of injustice in the world, and made its voice heard. The Society has welcomed into its ranks people of all races and national origins; in Kentucky, it purchased slaves to release them from bondage. Shaker sisters petitioned for justice in the Dreyfus affair; the Society took up collections for the victims of war and natural disaster; although not participating in elections themselves, Believers spoke out for women's suffrage and women's rights. In matters of conscience, Believers have been ready not only to express their views, but to suffer the consequences of their refusal to compromise principle —submitting to imprisonment, for example,

rather than attending military musters. Theirs has never been a faith of convenience.

"Shaker Birthdays"

IF THE CELEBRATIONS of the winters of Shaker life are solemn, those of summertime are joyful. Believers mark two birthdays each year, the anniversaries of their entrance into the world and of their "gathering" into the Society. Sister Mildred was brought to the Shakers at Alfred, Maine, in the summer of 1903. Her "Shaker birthday," observed each July by the members of the family and her friends, is a day of special happiness for the community. More than eighty years of her life have been spent among Believers, but the story of that first day at Alfred remains vivid in her mind.

I went to the Shakers on July 7, 1903, a very hot July day. I remember leaving Providence [Rhode Island] on the train early in the morning. It seemed to me I rode all day long and . . . I guess we must have ridden most of the day because I didn't get to Alfred until about five o'clock at night, when I was met there by one of the brethren with a horse and buggy—such was the transportation we used in those days!—and I was taken to the Trustees' Office (my mother also was with me) and we stayed there overnight. And in the morning Eldress Fannie Casey who was the Eldress at Alfred at the time . . . and by the way she also had been the one who was instrumental in taking me there, came down to the Office to see us and with her she brought Eldress Harriett Coolbroth from the Second Family at Alfred and . . . I had . . . become a little bit attached to Eldress Fannie, probably because I saw her first, and I was quite disturbed because she was going to send me down to the Second Family with Eldress Harriett . . . and, however, I was told to go so I went down to the Second Family. At that time there was just one little girl about my own age there and I was . . . I didn't seem to be very happy to start with and I remember sitting out back of the house on a swing, planning that when they weren't watching me so well and they got a little used to me and didn't know everything that I did, that I'd run down across the pasture and up over the mountain and go home to Providence. However, by the time they didn't watch me so well, I had changed my mind and I never did try that trip across the mountain! I grew very, very fond of Eldress Harriett. She was the mother that I needed and as a young child I thought that there couldn't possibly be anyone any lovelier.

All of the members of the family can tell stories about their own first experiences among Believers, stories that often are repeated at the celebration of "Shaker birthdays." Sister Elsie arrived at Sabbathday Lake in 1909, with her two younger twin sisters. Sister Laura Bailey took the twins into the Central Brick Dwelling to live with her there, but almost immediately found that they were too rambunctious for her. Little Elsie, who had spent her first night at Shaker Village in the Girls' Shop, was chosen in their stead and the very next day moved to the large dwelling. She lived there throughout her childhood, somewhat separate from the other children, and perhaps somewhat privileged. Brother Theodore's first encounter with Believers took place at Hancock in the mid 1950s. Having "read himself" into an acceptance of Shakerism, as he tells it, he went to visit the last functioning Shaker village in Massachusetts, only to find Hancock to be a sad, moribund place. He spoke separately to Brother Ricardo Belden, the community's last male member, and to Sister Mary F. Dahm, the local trustee. "Hearing of my interest in the life," Brother Ted often recalls,

each of them said to me, 'Go to Sabbathday Lake.' I went, and knew almost immediately that I wanted to spend my life there.

The Sixth of August

ANOTHER MAJOR summer celebration is held on August 6, the anniversary of the arrival of the first Shakers in North America in 1774. This day had long been observed as special in the Shaker calendar. Meeting in a spirit of thankfulness, the Shakers will retell the oft-repeated story of that eventful voyage, when Mother Ann and her companions brought their gospel to these shores.

It was in the spring of the year that James Whittaker received his vision of America that the faithful John Hocknell, at the request of Mother Ann, sought a vessel to convey the Shakers to the new world. The ship chosen by Hocknell was hardly seaworthy; according to one account, the *Mariah* was condemned, but Ann assured him "that God would not condemn it when we were in it." Having settled their affairs, Ann; her brother, William, and niece, Nancy; Hocknell and his son, Richard; James Whittaker; Mary Partington; James Shepherd; and, perhaps surprisingly, Ann's husband, Abraham, who then professed faith in the testimony, embarked at Liverpool on May 19, 1774, their passage having been paid for by Hocknell. The *Mariah*'s home port was New York; the vessel was in the charge of Captain Smith.

The long voyage on the high seas was eventful, giving rise to traditional stories that appear almost biblical in content and structure. Captain Smith and his crew were intolerant of the Shakers' preaching, especially when Mother Ann "felt constrained to testify against the wickedness of the seamen," and they were offended by their religious exercises. More than once, in apparent exasperation, the captain threatened to have them thrown overboard, but the small group of six men and three women continued to praise God in song and dance. To make matters worse, the vessel foundered in a terrible storm; its pumps were barely sufficient to keep it afloat. In the midst of the turbulence, the Shaker leader came to the captain and quietly reassured him. "Captain, be of good cheer," the traditional story supposes her to have said,

There shall not a hair of our heads perish; we shall arrive safe to America. I was just now sitting by the mast, and I saw a bright angel of God, through whom I received the promise.

With this assurance, the little band of Believers "put their hands to the pumps and encouraged the seamen." Soon afterward, the storm abated, a loose plank having been restored to its place

Mother

6. At Manchester, in England,
This blessed fire began,
And like a flame in stubble,
From house to house it ran:
A few at first receiv'd it,
And did their lusts forsake;
And soon their inward power
Brought on a mighty shake.

7. The rulers cried, "Delusion!
Who can these Shakers be?
Are these the wild fanatics,
Bewitched by *Ann Lee?*
We'll stop this noise and shaking
It never shall prevail;
We'll seize the grand deceiver,
And thrust her into jail."

8. Before their learned councils,
Though oft she was arraign'd,
Her life was uncondemned,
Her character unstain'd:
And by her painful travel,
Her suff'rings and her toil,
A little Church was formed
On the European soil.

9. This little band of union,
In apostolic life,
Remain'd awhile in England,
Among the sons of strife;
Till the Columbian Eagle,
Borne by an eastern breeze,
Convey'd this little Kingdom,
Across the rolling Seas.

10. To mark their shining passage,
Good angels flew before,
Towards the land of promise,
Columbia's happy shore.
Hail, thou victorious gospel!
And that auspicious day,
When Mother safely landed,
In Hudson's lovely bay!

11. Near Albany they settled,
And waited for a while,
Until a mighty shaking
Made all the desert smile.
At length a gentle whisper,
The tidings did convey,
And many flock'd to Mother,
To learn the living way.

12. Through storms of persecution,
The truth she did maintain,
And show'd how sin was conquer'd,
and how we're born again:
The old corrupted nature,
From place to place she trod,
And show'd a new creation,
The only way of God.

13. About four years she labour'd
With the attentive throng,
Confirm'd the young believers,
And helped their souls along.
At length she clos'd her labour,
And vanish'd out of sight,
And left the Church increasing,
In the pure gospel light.

14. How much are they deceived,
Who think that Mother's dead!
She lives among her offspring,
Who just begin to spread;
And in her outward order,
There's one supplies her room,
And still the name of *Mother,*
Is like a sweet perfume.

16. I love that testimony,
That shows me what to do;
I love my precious Mother,
I love the Elders too;
The Brethren and the Sisters,
I love them and their ways,
And In this loving spirit,
I mean to spend my days.

through the instrumentality of a "great wave." From this time until the *Mariah* reached its destination on August 6, 1774, the Believers were not molested in their worship.

The first "set song" to be sung by the Shakers as they gather at dusk in the old meetinghouse to celebrate the sixth of August is frequently one called "Mother," by Elder Richard McNemar, which was included in the Society's first printed hymnal, *Millennial Praises,* in 1812–13. In keeping with the length of many of the narrative or didactic hymns of the period, the song is long; there are sixteen stanzas in all. The Shakers generally sing ten of these (those reprinted on p. 123) at the August anniversary service. Its sprightly words summarize the church's beginnings in England, the voyage to America and the brief public ministry of Mother Ann. It is interesting to note how thoroughly comfortable Believers had become with a name originally given to them in derision by world. "Shaking" is now used as a metaphor for the faith experience of the church, not merely as a description of the physical exercise associated with its worship.

Shaker Spirituals

VERY SOON AFTER a visitor's introduction to Shaker Village, the importance of music in the life of the family becomes evident. The Shakers hold hundreds of songs in their collective consciousness, most of which have been transmitted from Believer to Believer in an unbroken tradition. Others have been learned anew from the many music manuscripts preserved in the Society's library, or from a creative interchange with such scholars as Daniel W. Patterson, much of whose research on Shaker music had been conducted at the Village. Songs express a multitude of emotions for Believers. The Shakers sing them spontaneously in work or worship, as the spirit moves them. Music also functions as a means of dialogue in Shaker meeting, often to the surprise of new visitors from the world.

All who worship with the Shakers are invited to stand at their place, if moved to do so, and to share a personal insight or response to the biblical lessons appointed for the day. (To allow sufficient preparation, the readings are posted on a small blackboard in the vestibule of the dwellinghouse two or three days prior to Sunday.) But while Shakers are encouraged to "labor" for a sense of consonance with the Gospel lesson, meeting is a time when any sentiment of the heart may be expressed openly. Brother Theodore Johnson is fond of quoting Mother Ann Lee, that "a strange gift never came from God," when he extends the community's invitation to guests to be "free" of undue reticence or shyness in meeting. It is a tribute to the vitality of the Shaker religious tradition that many visitors do respond, sometimes with an unrestrained openness more surprising to themselves, perhaps, than to the Believers. They speak of some concern or personal need, share their successes or failures, or ask for prayer or encouragement. Whatever doubt or need is expressed, the Shakers seem able to draw a song from their oral repertory that responds to it. One of the sisters or brethren will "pitch" a tune and the others will pick it up, as the community reaches out to express its caring concern.

Daniel W. Patterson, whose study of the Shaker musical tradition has spanned several decades, had estimated that between eight thousand and ten thousand Shaker songs, some with as many as forty variant forms, are preserved in the surviving manuscript collections alone, an extraordinary number, considering the limited population of the societies. Indeed, Shaker music may comprise the largest separate folk music tradition in the United States. Many of the earliest tunes were drawn from secular folk music, but the texts, with relatively few exceptions, are by Believers. The central role of singing in the Society and the increasing tendency of the Shakers to shield their communities from worldly influences after the first two decades of their history, however, led to the unself-conscious creation of a distinctive music in several genres. Although the songs frequently were recorded by Shaker scribes, using a unique form of "letteral" musical notation, in which the letters of the alphabet rather than standard round notes

Shaker family singing and "motioning" a spiritual

were utilized, they carry the hallmarks of an authentic folk tradition.

One of the most accomplished composers at Sabbathday Lake was Elder Oliver Holmes, who entered the community as a child with his parents, Simeon and Mercy Weston Holmes, in 1785. In her commonplace book, which is a rich source of community lore, Sister Aurelia recorded how Elder Oliver taught one of his anthems to the brethren.

The young brethren were all there learning the anthem and did not mean to have the sisters know any thing about it, and so spring a surprise on them the next Sabbath,—But one of the little boys went into the kitchen where the sisters were, to get a pitcher of water.

—He could not keep a secret.—He says, 'They are making anthems out to the brethren's shop, and they have got eyes like flames of fire.'

So the sisters were all prepared for the anthem next Sabbath.

Elder Oliver's anthem was "The Faithful Witness," which was published in 1852 by Elder Henry Blinn of Canterbury, New Hampshire, as the first composition in his *Sacred Repository of Anthems and Hymns, for Devotional Worship and Praise*. Its opening words, "These things saith the Son of God, who hath his eyes like unto a flame of fire," were no doubt the source of the little Shaker boy's allusion.

Although the regular practice of dancing or marching in worship was discontinued at Sabbathday Lake in 1903, many of the songs still current in the oral repertory were originally intended to accompany the dance. Even the later, more formal music of the printed hymnals is marked to indicate which are "marches" or "slow marches." Sister Aurelia Mace left an account of the exercises in her commonplace book. Among them were

[a] regular march, with a motion of the hands held at right angles with the elbow, palms down—another form called the bowing march, slower—carrying the hands down to the side on each measure of the song, bending the body slightly foward.—These forms of worship were in vogue in the Society at Gloucester more than eighty years—though sometime in the '50's the form was changed, turning the palms of hands upward and so it continued until the marchers were closed together in a circle. Brethren two by two and sisters following two by two. Or sometimes following in the rows as they assembled, back and forth, across the room.

They also kept up the stepping manner, which was introduced by Father Joseph Meacham. He saw that form by vision in the third heavens, and taught it to the people. Two steps up and three taps, and two steps back and three taps. Sometimes taking the back-step shuffle—straight rows across the rooms, brethren and sisters on their own sides respectively.—This was called the "Holy Order."

Towards the close of the meeting they would sing quick songs and the people would dance, each like a living spark, as David danced before the ark.—Brethren and sisters on their own sides of the house. In this quick dance would almost always come the inspiration, and, heavenly gifts would be manifested from the spirit land.

The Shakers still "motion" or pantomime certain songs, using traditional gestures and movements in place. The maintenance and transmission of these traditions at Sabbathday Lake has been a special emphasis in the leadership of Sister Mildred, who learned them from Eldress Harriett Coolbroth, Sister Lucinda Taylor and others at Alfred. Indeed, at Alfred, the practice of marching in worship was taught to the children and young folk until about 1930. Several years ago, Sister Mildred recorded her early memories of learning the traditional music of the Society from the older sisters.

. . . I learned a great many [songs] from Eldress Harriet Coolbroth, and as I grew older, we used to learn quite a number from Sister Lucinda Taylor. At the laundry, we used to get her into the ironing room and get her up on one of the big ironing tables. When she got older, she was about eighty-five, eighty-six years old then, we'd ask her to sing songs to us. She was kind of shy. She'd say, "Oh, you don't want me to sing to you." We'd say, "We do, we do! We want to learn a song." And she'd teach us songs . . . And then we'd get her to show us some of the early dances, which we never saw, and one special one that was most beautiful was "The Heavenly Father's March," which she could do. She was so graceful, and she had a voice just like a bird. A beautiful voice, even at that extreme age. . . . From then on I went on to learn every song that I could. I couldn't learn them from the books because I didn't understand the letteral notation which was the Shakers' way of noting the songs in the manuscripts, and so we just learned them from hearing other people sing them.

In 1983, the National Endowment for the Arts and the Smithsonian Institution awarded Sister Mildred a National Heritage Fellowship as "the principal conservator of the Shaker song tradition." The citation read in part:

Born in 1897, Sister Mildred Barker is now the spiritual leader of the Shaker Society in Maine. She is a person of remarkable musical gifts with a fine musical memory and a thorough knowledge of the Shaker repertory and song style. She also knows how to pantomime Shaker hymns, a custom practiced by few Shaker singers today.

The services of Sister Mildred Barker have been outstanding in fostering the song tradition of the Shaker community, documenting it for posterity, and sharing it freely with the outside world.

Simple Gifts

Transcription by Daniel W. Patterson

'Tis the gift to be sim-ple, 'tis the gift to be free; 'Tis the

gift to come down where we ought to be; And

when we find our-selves in the place just right, 'Twill

be in the val-ley of love and de-light. When true sim-

plic-i-ty is gaind, To bow and to bend we

shan't be a-sham'd To turn, turn will be our de-light, 'Till by

turn - ing, turn - ing we come round right.

'Tis the gift to be simple,
'Tis the gift to be free;
'Tis the gift to come down
where we ought to be;
And when we find ourselves in the place
just right,
'Twill be in the valley of love and delight.
When true simplicity is gained,
To bow and to bend we shan't be asham'd.
To turn, turn will be our delight,
'Till by turning, turning
we come around right.

It is only in the twentieth century that this widespread public recognition of the extraordinary richness of the Shaker music tradition has emerged, although it became common in the last century for visitors to the important hotels and spas at Lebanon Springs, New York; Lenox, Massachusetts; and Poland Spring, Maine, to include a stop at Shaker public meeting in their holiday plans to observe Shaker worship in music and dance. What, for the Believers, was a means of celebrating union with the Infinite, became for the world the object of a day's outing in the country. In the modern period, however, there has been a serious response to the heritage. Doris Humphrey created "The Shakers," a dance choreographed from traditional music in 1931 and originally entitled, "Dance of the Chosen." "Appalachian Spring" was composed as a dance suite for Martha Graham by Aaron Copland in 1943–44, utilizing a series of variations on the famous Shaker spiritual, "Simple Gifts," by Elder Joseph Brackett (see p. 127), originally of the little Shaker family at Gorham, Maine, and later elder of the church at Sabbathday Lake and senior member of the Maine ministry. Elder Otis wrote of Elder Joseph's "remarkable and natural gift to sing by which he would often fill a whole assembly with the quickening power of God." The last of the Gorham Shakers, he died on July 4, 1882, at the age of eighty-five years.

During the Era of Mother's Work, gifted Shaker "instruments" received hundreds of

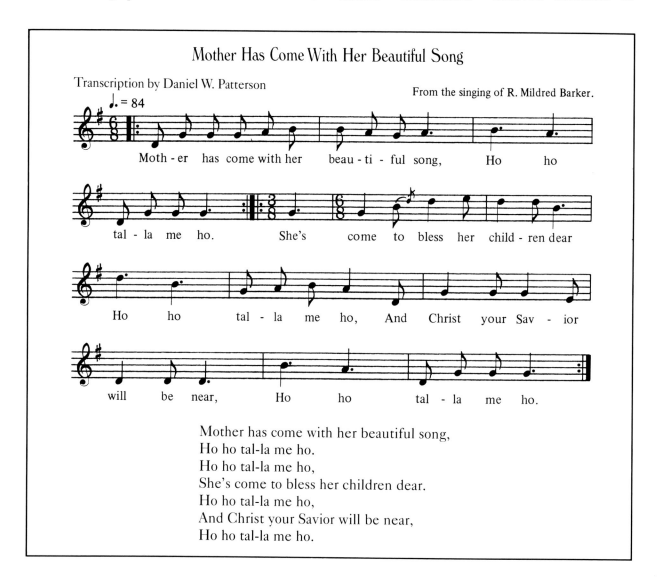

Mother Has Come With Her Beautiful Song

Transcription by Daniel W. Patterson

From the singing of R. Mildred Barker.

Mother has come with her beautiful song,
Ho ho tal-la me ho.
Ho ho tal-la me ho,
She's come to bless her children dear.
Ho ho tal-la me ho,
And Christ your Savior will be near,
Ho ho tal-la me ho.

Family at work, kitchen of Central Brick Dwelling

Dresses on clothesline

songs, some of which were cast in "unknown tongues." Many of these "gift songs" survive in the oral repertory at Sabbathday Lake. Even after the period of manifestations came to an end, however, Believers in the bishopric of Maine would continue to receive songs by inspiration. Sister Mildred often sings one of these, "Mother Has Come With Her Beautiful Song," by Paulina Springer. It is said that Sister Paulina learned the song at Alfred from a little bird in 1887 (See p. 128).

Shaker Clothing

SUMMER VISITORS to public meeting at Sabbathday Lake during the nineteenth century frequently commented upon the dress of the sisters and brethren. A reporter for the *Lewiston* (Maine) *Journal* attended worship services at the community on a summer's Sunday in 1881. When he arrived, he saw the Shakers "in their dignified drab coat-tails, and Shakeresses in their neat, plain gowns, glistening white-pointed kerchiefs, and their scrupulously starched bonnets," marching from the dwellinghouse to the old church across the way. He was especially moved by a Shaker lad "of perhaps ten summers," who wore a loose cherry-colored "sacque" and a "high-buttoned velveteen waistcoat," and by a young brother in a "plum-colored" coat.

The dress observed by the Lewiston reporter was a simple and functional adaptation of the clothing commonly worn in rural New York and New England during the late eighteenth century. Within a few years of the organization of the United Society, the Shakers began to produce textiles within their communities. For the sake of efficiency in production as well as for "union" among the members, a degree of uniformity soon prevailed. Although there is continuing evidence that the Shaker leadership allowed for the expression of at least some personal taste (in matters of color, for example), the practical need to limit production to a reasonable number of colors, fabric types and designs, limited the choices available to the Believers.

Not all visitors to Shaker Village were as impressed by Shaker clothing as the reporter for the *Lewiston Journal*. Three years later, in 1884, another reporter visiting the community commented in an article in the *People's News* that the costume of the Shaker sisters was less than beautiful. Sister Aurelia wrote a letter to the editor in defense of the people she loved.

Yesterday was Sunday, and the "little church" was crowded. Many came from Poland Spring, two miles distant on the north. Auburn, Lewiston and Portland were also represented in the audience. All here to witness the worship of this peculiar people. Why peculiar? Because they have dared to differ from others. In looking around at the people who filled our church, we could not help observing how many there were who saw us only in the light in which we were viewed by the lady whose letter appeared in your Saturday's paper. But there was a class there who saw things differently—who saw nobility and dignity in the Shaker brethren, who saw loveliness and beauty in the Shaker sisters' dress, which was not, my friend, "selected with a view to its ugliness;" that is a mistake, but with a view to utility and comfort. "Your tastes are perverted," said our good Elder Frederick Evans to one who failed to see beauty in the Shaker sisters' dress. "Bad diet has done it, or you have been wrongly educated."

During the nineteenth century, the design of the clothing worn by the sisters and brethren evolved into a distinctive "Shaker" style, that varied with the seasons or according to the function for which it was intended (e.g., work clothes or Sabbath dress). The most notable feature of the sisters' dress were the shoulder kerchief or "cape" and the close-fitting linen or cotton cap and bonnet of palm-leaf or woven straw. The brethren wore a long surcoat and wide-brimmed hat.

By the end of the nineteenth century, the Shakers began to purchase textiles from the world, rather than producing them within the communities. Before long, "world's clothing" could be found in use in the villages, as well. In 1896, the eldresses of the central ministry at Mount Lebanon, New York, visited Sabbathday Lake and gave "liberty" for the sisters "to take

Shaker bonnet

off their caps." But, as Sister Aurelia noted in the official Church Record, "our sisters like their caps so well that they will not avail themselves of it. *Not Yet.*" Indeed, the cap was worn at Sabbathday Lake well into the twentieth century. Sister Mildred continues to wear her cap on special occasions.

Today, the sisters at Sabbathday Lake wear an adaptation of the nineteenth-century dress. Although the dress fabric is purchased from the world, a "cape" or yoke continues to be worn. The brethren of the community frequently wear the smocklike Shaker shirt that was a feature of the brethren's work clothing during the last century.

Friends of the Shakers

A MAJOR SUMMER EVENT at Sabbathday Lake is the annual gathering of the Friends of the Shakers, a national organization that assists the community in its efforts to preserve the material heritage of the Society. The occasion is frequently associated with the sixth of August; it was in 1974 at the 200th anniversary celebration of the events of that day that the group had its beginnings. The four-day 1974 bicentennial observance was a profoundly moving experience for the Shakers and participants from the world alike. The old church held more people than at any time since the closing of public meetings in the late nineteenth century. Sister Frances wrote to a young friend how impressive it was to see everyone coming together in tribute to the little band that arrived from England on August 6, 1774. "One of the pictures in my mind," she wrote,

is the sight of all those people . . . all around the Meeting House lawn and lined up along the white picket fence. It was a lovely sight: happy people, hushed in almost a reverent sort of way . . . [and there was] the singing in which somehow everyone took part even though they did not know the songs . . .

The Friends of the Shakers have returned to Sabbathday Lake each year since the memorable sixth of August celebrations in 1974. Brothers Theodore and Arnold generally arrange a special exhibition from the museum collections at Sabbathday Lake for the occasion, based on the theme chosen for the weekend gathering, and there are special lectures, singing meetings, a picnic on the shores of the lake, and the regular Shaker meeting for worship on Sunday morning. The friends take a particular interest in the museum. With thousands of others each summer, they are drawn to exhibitions featuring the spare but elegant Shaker furniture and ingenious small crafts, colorful textiles and historic artifacts. Even after many visits, they marvel at Shaker inventions like the "tilter chair," a chair fitted with a button joint or ball-and-socket device that permits the sitter to tilt the chair backward with very little risk of tipping over or damaging floors (a patent for this device was issued to Brother George O. Donnell of New Lebanon in 1852); Shaker architectural conventions like the space-saving built-in cases of drawers and cupboards that line the walls of many rooms or the ubiquitous pegboard or rail that allows almost everything, including chairs, to be hung, out of the way, when not in use; or the beautiful, other-worldly products of the Era of Mother's Work, the gift drawings of Eldress Hester Ann Adams and Sister Polly Collins, graphic evocations of the spirit-land believed to have been received by inspiration in the 1840s and 1850s, two of the community's treasures.

The Shaker Aesthetic

THE DEVELOPMENT OF Shaker design, whether in architecture or furniture, represented a continuing interplay between the motives of simplicity and perfection—two ideals that have their origin in the teachings of Mother Ann herself. The Shakers received the vernacular forms common to their region and period and altered them

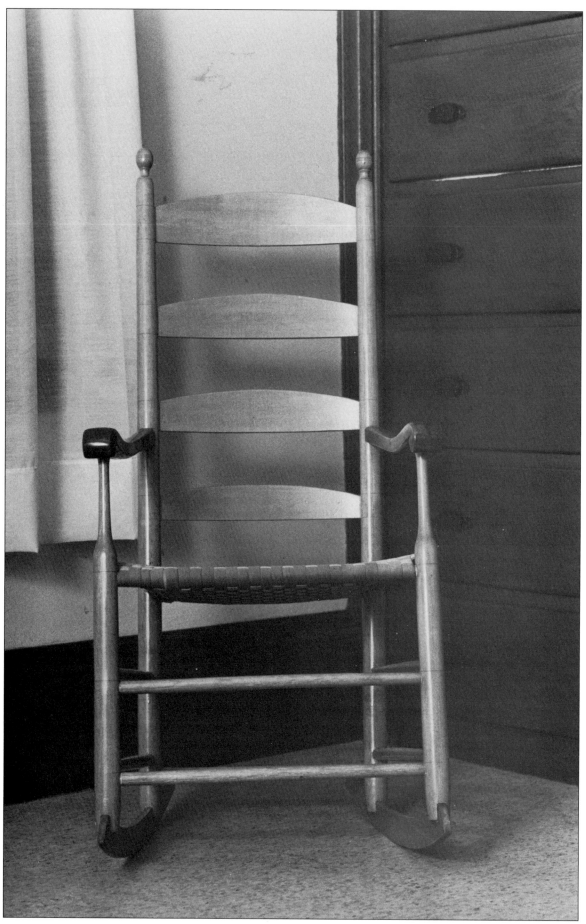

Shaker rocker, maple with natural stain, Alfred,
Maine, ca. 1850

to suit a developing community aesthetic. In the early days of the church, new Believers brought their own furniture and household effects with them and donated them for community use. From this stock of communal property came the models for the first furniture created within the Society. Before long, the needs of large-scale communities required furniture forms not readily available outside the villages—long dining tables, ample cases of drawers for storage, tailoring counters and the like.

The earliest furniture produced by the Shakers of Maine shared many of the characteristics of the country cabinetry of the day. As Brother Theodore Johnson has noted, "Primitive Maine Shaker furniture may be characterized as substantial, even heavy, yet vigorous and eminently practical. It bears all the marks of the Maine soil to which its creators' lives were so firmly attached. Pieces of the period are . . . most commonly made of pine or of maple. Obviously Maine joiners of the period saw little beauty in the natural wood itself, for virtually all [early] pieces . . . are painted or color-stained. An in-

digo-based blue, mustard yellow, a dark forest green, and a variety of shades of red are the predominant colors."

As the communities developed, and Believers became more certain of the nature of their call to the "gospel life," Shaker cabinetmakers and joiners attempted in their work to capture the essence of the Shaker way. Beginning in the 1820s and lasting approximately to the 1860s, the "classic era" in Shaker design saw the production of the lean, elegant, profoundly beautiful furniture forms that we associate with the Shakers: Shaker chairs and rocker; tall cupboards and cases of drawers; trestle tables; simple, well-proportioned candle stands; trustees' desks; washstands; and other forms, all demonstrating the artistry of their makers. During the classic period, painted surfaces were not as common, the craftsmen preferring to highlight the natural color of the wood. In addition to pine and maple, chestnut, birch, cherry and other fruitwoods were frequently used. Elder Elisha Pote and other Maine Shaker cabinetmakers occasionally used contrasting woods or varied natural with

Sewing room, Ministry's Shop. The pine and birch sewing desks are a matched pair made for Eldresses Fannie Casey and Mary Walker by Elder Henry Green of Alfred, Maine, ca. 1890

Nineteenth-century Shaker bedroom, Sabbathday Lake museum

stained or painted surfaces in their work.

After the Civil War, Maine craftsmen such as Elders Henry Green of Alfred and Delmer Wilson of Sabbathday Lake continued the tradition of furniture design, although a certain late-Victorian sensibility and interest in ornamentation are evident in their efforts.

The Sabbathday Lake Shakers take justifiable pride in the evidences of their material heritage abounding in the Village. But they are quick to emphasize that this heritage is a product of their faith and cannot be understood except in relation to their way of life and its underlying motives. In a recent interview, Sister Mildred emphasized the need for this understanding:

People look in upon us and that's the first thing they say. "Oh, they're the people that made that nice furni- ture, *they made nice chairs and tables." And I say, "I know it, I almost expect to be remembered as a chair or a table." But the people that come in feeling that way, they forget there's something special behind that work. There's the religion that produced the good chairs and the good tables, because everything they put their hand to was well done.*

The Trustees' Office

MANY SUMMER VISITORS stop at the Village store, located in the Trustees' Office, which is open for business six days a week. The Shakers built the structure in 1816 at the request of Mother Lucy Wright, who perceived a need for

Shaker cupboard

a residence for the aged members of the community during her visit to New Gloucester in that year. It did not serve as Trustees' Office until 1880. Prior to that time, a building raised in 1796 that was located south of the Village's current cinder-block garage was used for that purpose. It later served as the hired men's residence and in 1957, was taken down, board by board, and moved to The Shaker Museum, Old Chatham, New York.

The location of the Village store within the Trustees' Office is a customary feature of Shaker community organization. For many years, until well into the twentieth century, the Shakers received callers from the world and conducted business with outsiders only at the office. Except under special circumstances, visitors were not freely admitted to other community buildings. Under the supervision of office deacons and deaconesses, or trustees, who resided there, the Trustees' Office was the point of connection between the Village and the world. In accordance with the provisions of the Covenant of the United Society, the trustees hold title to all church properties for the benefit of the members as a whole. They also keep the Society's books of account, manage mercantile operations and business transactions, and take charge of legal and financial matters. The Shaker post office, until it closed its operations in 1955, was located at the office, Sister Eleanor Philbrook (1899–1976) serving as the last Shaker postmistress. Today, Sister R. Mildred Barker, the Society's senior trustee, divides her time between the office, where much business with the world continues to be conducted, and the Central Brick Dwelling, where she attends to other obligations. Sister Mildred also manages the Shaker Store, assisted by Sister Marie Burgess and "extended family" member Ruth Nutter.

At the turn of the century, Sister Aurelia entertained many prominent guests in her sitting

Brothers Ted and Arnold at work

room at the Trustees' Office. Most of them came to the Village from the nearby Poland Spring House, a famous summer resort, with whose owners the Shakers maintained particularly close and affectionate relations. If Aurelia received wealthy and respected guests from the Springs, she never turned away a poor traveler, either. Indeed, the sign outside her door announced, "Trustees' Office. Visitors are Always Welcome." In the summer of 1900, an aged man, looking weary and worn, his clothing torn, rang the bell of the office. According to the well-known story, Sister Aurelia welcomed him warmly, offered him some lemonade and invited him to stay for the noon meal. When it came time to leave, the old man was sent on his way with sandwiches, doughnuts, apple pie and some grape jelly. Although Aurelia did not know it at the time, the man was Charles L. Tiffany, patron of the arts and founder of the famous jewelry firm, who had lost his way on a morning stroll through the woods and fields between the Poland Spring House and Shaker Village. According to a newspaper report of the time, when the other elegantly dressed guests at the hotel sat down for dinner that evening,

Mr. Tiffany and another rich New Yorker slipped away, walked to the shore of the lake, spread Sister Aurelia's lunch on a flat rock and ate every crumb of it.

Several days later, Sister Aurelia received a package, containing a set of silver spoons, each marked "Aurelia." A card was enclosed:

> In return for the kindness you showed me after my encounter with the blackberry brambles last week.
>
> Charles Tiffany

Transacting business with the world placed Shaker trustees, especially brethren, under a great burden during the nineteenth century. Frequently required to travel and spend considerable time outside of the protecting wings of the community, they were occasionally importuned with improvident transactions or subjected to the temptations of the world. Aside from the ordinary vicissitudes of commercial endeavor (as when the firm of Nutter & Kimball, to whom all the oak shooks manufactured in the community in 1878 were sold, tottered on the brink of bankruptcy and subjected the Shakers to a loss of $4,000) there were cases of unlawful loans or investments or even of downright dishonesty. In 1860, the central ministry removed Ransom Gilman from the Society at New Gloucester and placed him at the Second Family, New Lebanon after he had incurred heavy debt that placed a great burden on the family. Several years later, Brother Charles Vining, who had charge of the Society's gristmill in the 1860s, left the community after speculating in wheat and flour and plunging the family into debt. These and other cases created substantial losses at Sabbathday Lake, which were felt for years to come. But they were exceptions. Most who have been called to the trusteeship of the Society have been true to their trust of great care and responsibility.

Summer Produce and Sales

IN SUMMERS PAST, teams of brethren and sisters traveled to resorts throughout New England and along the Atlantic Coast as far south as Cape May, New Jersey, selling the sisters' sale work and other products of community shops. Until the retirement in 1957 of Sister Eva Libby, who went on these summer selling trips for fifty years, both from her home at Alfred and, after 1931, at Sabbathday Lake, the arrival of the Shakers was a common phenomenon in oceanside and mountain resorts. With the cooperation of the management of the hotel, the Shakers would set up a table to attractively display their wares—woven poplar sewing boxes and jewelry cases, oval carriers fitted with emeries, wax, pincushions and needle books, fir balsam pillows, horsehair sieves, splint baskets, imported dolls dressed in handmade Shaker costumes, horsehair brushes, hooked and woven plush rugs, and knitted and crocheted fancy goods. Beginning in the last third of the nineteenth century and

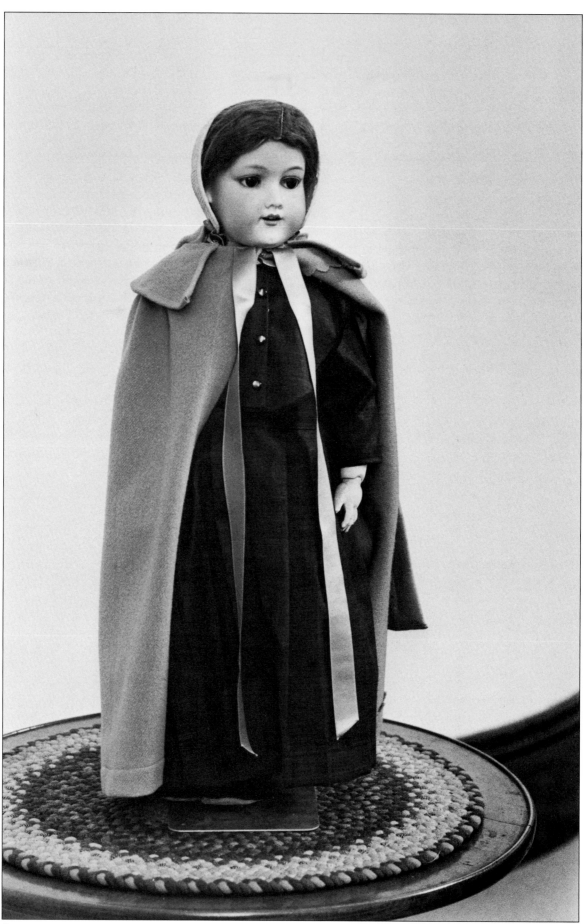

Doll in traditional Shaker dress

throughout the first half of the twentieth, summer sales of sisters' work were an important element in the economic base of the Society. The Ricker family, which owned the nearby Poland Spring House, was always ready to oblige the Believers, too, and groups of Shaker sisters would often be found there, sitting behind a lovely display of the excellent work of their hands.

During the summer season, the gardens of the community begin to yield their rich bounty. Fresh vegetables dominate community meals, the cooks drawing upon a large store of traditional recipes. In fact, the practice of vegetarianism has had a long and interesting history in the Shaker societies. For many Shaker leaders in the mid- and late-nineteenth century, refraining from eating meat was but a natural extension of their church's witness against violence and its sense of the sanctity of all life. Elder Frederick Evans and Eldress Anna White of the North Family, Mount Lebanon, urged the adoption of vegetarianism not only on these grounds, but for purposes of health as well; and the columns of the Society's monthly periodical, published from 1871 through 1899 under various names, frequently were given over to this subject. In some families, separate tables were set for vegetarians. In Maine, however, the practice never held sway, although the inclusion of fresh vegetables, often seasoned with herbs, is a staple of the community menus at Sabbathday Lake today. Sister Frances likes this recipe for salad.

Sabbathday Lake
Stringbean and Mushroom Salad
Mint Vinegar Dressing

1 pound string beans
¼ pound mushrooms
6 leaves unblemished Boston lettuce, or any available green

Cook string beans until just tender in boiling water. Drain and cool. Line six salad plates with lettuce and divide beans among the plates. Just before serving, slice mushrooms and arrange over beans. Serve with mint vinegar dressing. Serves 6.

Mint Vinegar Dressing

½ cup (4 oz.) mint vinegar
1 cup (8 oz.) olive oil
1 cup (8 oz.) vegetable oil
Salt and freshly ground pepper
1 teaspoon fresh mint, chopped (or ½ teaspoon dried)

Blend all ingredients together.

Picking strawberries

One of several nineteenth-century watercolor Village views by Elder Joshua
Bussell of Alfred, Maine, in the collections of the Sabbathday Lake Shakers

A variety of luscious berries also grace community tables during summer. Going berrying has always been a popular spring and summer pastime for the young folks at Sabbathday Lake and Alfred. Blueberries, blackberries and raspberries grow wild on the Shaker lands, and strawberries have long been cultivated in community gardens. Here is a favorite summer dessert recipe, as prepared by Sister Frances.

Strawberry Summer Pudding

½ loaf thin sliced white bread
1 quart ripe strawberries
¾ to 1 cup sugar (depending upon sweetness of berries)

Remove crusts from bread. Mash and sweeten berries. Line pan or mold with foil or waxed paper, place slices of bread on the bottom. Spoon mashed berries over the slices—and alternate berries and bread until pan is filled. Cover with waxed paper and cardboard cut slightly smaller than the pan and weight as evenly as possible. Chill at least 8 hours or overnight. For serving invert on a platter, top with whipped cream and scatter fresh berries around the pudding.

Serves 6–8 persons.

Other Summer Activities

SUMMER IS A colorful season in Shaker Village. Flowers and flowering plants abound in all their pretty hues. Early in Shaker history, Believers did not cultivate flowers for ornamental purposes only but grew varieties having a specific utility, such as the roses used in the preparation of rose water. During the late nineteenth century, the cultivation of flowers for sale by the sisters of the community became an important Village activity. Eldress Elizabeth Noyes and Sister Ada Cummings played a major role in floriculture at Shaker Village. The sisters planted large fields of tea roses, carnation pinks, asters, sweet peas, dahlias and other varieties, selling young plants in the spring and flowers in the summer. They also became expert in arranging corsages, bouquets and floral centerpieces to grace the tables at the Poland Spring House. In November 1895, the young boys of the community built a hothouse to grow tomato and celery plants. Eldress Lizzie paid two-fifths of the $65.12 in materials required for the structure and reserved a similar portion of the facility for the sisters to cultivate flowers during the colder months of the year, as well.

The fullness of summer imposes a substantial amount of work on the members of the community. Farm and gardens require tending, the business of the Society has to be conducted and a steady stream of visitors demands attention. Brothers Arnold and Wayne seem always to be on the move, attending first to one chore and then another. The days are surprisingly warm; indeed, the temperature and humidity of a hot August day at Sabbathday Lake make work very difficult. Summer is haying season and much energy is expended in the effort. In a recent season the Society harvested 4,080 bales or sixty tons of hay, much of it sold in the field. But there is occasionally some time for summer recreation. An entry in the official "Church Record" for July 27, 1896, indicates that life at Shaker Village always had its light moments:

Brethren try to ride the bicycle. Some of them succeed quite well in learning. It is good as a circus to the Sisters to watch them.

The lake beckons, as well, and the younger members of the family frequently make their way to it for a swim in the early evening, when its waters glisten in the moonlight. The lake has a sad story attached to it. In 1897, a fourteen-year-old girl, Annie Dorrington, who had entered the Society as a child of six years in 1888, drowned in the lake, apparently intending to take her own life. The community was stunned. An intelligent youngster who was being educated to serve as a teacher at the Shaker school, Annie was well loved by the sisters who had charge of the Girls' Order. An official inquiry found no evidence of wrongdoing on the part of the Shakers; indeed, a large, happy group of children then resided in the community. But the waste of this young life deeply affected the Shakers.

By the end of summer, there is a discernible difference at Shaker Village. One by one, the members of the extended summer family return to their homes; teenage tour guides to prepare for school, adults to pick up the threads of their own lives. Tourists continue to visit, if in somewhat smaller numbers, and members of the family must be pressed into service in the reception center and museum, as needed. Fewer people sit down at the dinner table, and the talk in the dining room is less animated, more reflective. The color of the Village begins to change, too;

soon after the family picnic on Labor Day, the deep green of shade trees gives way to subtle traces of red and gold. Days are shorter and nights cooler, and change is in the air. Reflecting on the coming change, Sister Ada Cummings mused in her "Notes about Home" in the September 1895 issue of *The Manifesto*, that

[d]uring the busy summer we have striven to maintain the Cause of Truth and now as it is already waning we wish to keep our spirits alive, and not let the Testimony of God wane within our own souls.

The sun may wane, the stars go down,
And reign of time be o'er;
But the living light in the heart that's pure,
Shall shine forever more.

IV · FALL

Over the meadows of golden grain,
The sound of the reaper has passed again;
The flush of the summer has faded away,
On the silent wing of harvesting day.
Beautiful leaves await our feet,
Even as we their glory meet;
Gifts of the Father and Mother are here,
In the bountiful crops that crown the year.

"Autumn Song"
from *Shaker Music:
Original Inspirational Hymns
and Songs* (New York, 1884)

SHAKER LORE IS RESONANT WITH THE metaphor of autumn. As you walk the paths of Shaker Village in early October, the profoundly beautiful display of the season is all about you, in the trees and in the the fields. The colors change every day, from brilliant reds and yellows to warm purples, gold and browns. It is not difficult to understand the impress of autumn on the Shaker consciousness, as you stand amid its glory.

Autumn Harvests

IN THE VILLAGE, harvesting activities are very much in evidence throughout the early autumn. In the old days, the brethren and their hired men dug hundreds of bushels of potatoes and picked apples by the thousands during the season, in addition to harvesting corn, wheat, oats and the produce of the family's gardens. Although the village apple orchards are now leased to an outsider, the young brethren must still harvest the herb and vegetable gardens. Whatever is not needed by the family is offered for sale. Much of the produce retained by the family is canned. Autumn is the time for preserving and for cider making, too. The kitchen and storeroom of the Central Brick Dwelling are redolent with the sweet scent of apples during October and November.

When Brother Delmer Wilson had charge of the orchards earlier in this century, and the production of apples was a major Village enterprise, he built and installed a mechanical apple grader in the first floor of the Village's 1824 Herb House, where the fruit was graded and packed for sale. Current production is in excess of 12,500 bushels each year and many baskets of apples find their way to the family for its own use.

During the second half of the nineteenth century, the Sabbathday Lake Shakers cut and dried huge quantities of apples each autumn for pies and other desserts, but especially for the famous Shaker applesauce. Sometimes an apple-paring bee would be organized, in which the children

participated, to accomplish the task of paring and slicing. At other times, the responsibility was assumed by one person, as when Brother Jacob Fasting cut 1,220 pounds of "nice and white" apples for drying in a couple of days in October 1876. Applesauce is a product traditionally associated with several Shaker communities; today's collectors prize the wooden firkins in which it was put up and sold in the nineteenth century. But this delicious old-fashioned Shaker delight is not the applesauce we generally are familiar with today. Here is Sister Ethel Peacock's recipe.

Shaker Applesauce

2 pounds dried apple slices
1/3 gallon water
2/3 gallon cider, boiled down from
2 gallons fresh cider
1/2 pound sugar (optional)

Soak apples overnight in water. In the morning add the boiled-down cider to the soaked apples. Cover tightly and simmer for 3½ hours; add sugar, if desired. Do not stir, for the apple slices should remain whole and float in the rich, dark syrup.

Ardent Spirits and Tobacco

PERHAPS BECAUSE THE simplicity of their way of life implies a healthy moderation in all things, the Shakers have been tolerant in matters of food and drink. Although Shaker leaders wrestled with the question of allowing "ardent spirits" among Believers from time to time during the nineteenth century, and occasionally forbade or limited its use, the frequency with which the issue was debated is indicative of a mild and forbearing approach. One mid-nineteenth-century codification of rules, for example, suggested that the "younger class" of Believers, who pre-

Sister Marie with the last harvest of the season

Sister Marie and Brother Wayne

sumably had not become accustomed to the practice, abstain from ardent spirits, while the "older class" moderate their consumption. But for all Believers, especially in the summer, these rules very tolerantly allowed a "small beer." This is in keeping with the Shaker idea that simplicity does not require a cold or unmitigated asceticism, even in a celibate Society. For Believers, this is not a contradiction of terms. As Mother Lucy Wright suggested in the first quarter of the nineteenth century,

How much easier it is to live in a cheerful, joyous spirit that is refreshing to both body and soul, than to let a heavy, moody feeling prevail.

Autumn is cider time and, with their neighbors in the world, Shakers looked forward to the fermented variety, one suspects, as much as the sweet. This twentieth-century adaptation of a simple cider recipe has been a seasonal favorite at Sabbathday Lake.

The Brethren's Cider

1 fifth Lairds Apple Jack
¹⁄₂ gallon apple cider
Lemon peel

Mix apple jack and cider in punch bowl. Add ice. Serve straight up with a piece of lemon peel. Drink must be served cold.

Serves 15.

A similar concession had been made toward smoking or chewing tobacco. Though the practice was discountenanced in the nineteenth century after its unhealthful properties were recognized, the leadership somewhat begrudgingly continued to tolerate it, especially in the older brethren. An entry in the official New Gloucester Church Record for 1880, for example, lists the well-loved Elder Joseph Brackett and five other brethren—Abner Douglas, Paul Nowell, Thomas Noyes, George Clark and William Paul—as "guilty of the pernicious practice" of using tobacco, but states that they had agreed to be satisfied with one-half pound per month: "Brother William Dumont," the entry states,

is appointed comissary to get the vile weed at the Office and distribute it to the Brethren on the first day of every month.

For those who were able to give up the practice, however, the Shakers had only praise. Soon after Brother Granville Merrill entered the Society in 1868, he abandoned the use of tobacco, taking a solemn pledge that he would never again return to the practice. After several years as a Believer, Brother Granville became ill and it seemed certain that he was dying. There were some in the family who thought that the withdrawal from his old habit might have been too great a shock to his system, and suggested that he take a little tobacco again. His reply was recorded approvingly by Sister Aurelia.

"Nay," said he, "I will never put another piece of tobacco into my mouth." "Not if you know it would save your life?," said Eldress Hester Ann Adams. "Not if I knew it would save my life," was his answer. "I will keep the promise I have made to God."

Granville Merrill was only thirty-nine years of age when he died on July 4, 1878, deeply mourned by his brethren and sisters in the gospel. For many years the striking of an ingenious outdoor clock that Granville built himself and installed in the south attic of the brethren's shop was an hourly reminder of his talent and dedication.

It was not only the brethren who used tobacco. As Eldress Anna White and Sister Leila S. Taylor observed in *Shakerism: Its Meaning and Message,* "many an older Shaker saint rested and consoled herself with her pipe." The two Sisters preserved this wonderfully characteristic story of how a Believer at New Lebanon, New York, gave up the practice.

One of these smoking sisters, a humorous, steadfast soul, was Nancy Lockwood, whose spirit was . . . quaintly wise and full of sunshine. She thoroughly believed that the cross was the source of real happiness, for she had "proved it." The following incident is a sample of the way in which she met life. She had just seated herself in the spinning shop to enjoy an after dinner smoke, when someone casually remarked that the Ministry wished that all the sisters, who could, would give up smoking. Sister Nancy looked at her pipe and said to herself, "What do I smoke for? I never thought of it before. Is it because other people have the habit? Is it only an indulgence that I have practiced since I was a child?" Who or what answered her, she never told, but she arose and, extinguishing the tobacco, deposited her old pipe on a beam over her work place, saying, "There! You stay there till I take you down." There she worked for many years, with the token of her conquest before her eyes. With a twinkle in her eye that lighted her whole face, she was wont to end the story with "After that, I used my mouth for glad and heavenly songs instead of smoke." Years later, when the old spinning shop was torn down, there lay Nancy's pipe in its resting place on the beam.

Canning and Preserving

CANNING AND PRESERVING are fall activities at Sabbathday Lake, the produce of the family gardens being put up for use later in the year. Brother Samuel Kendrick, caretaker of the Boys' Order and village postmaster in the late nineteenth century, supervised the production of pickles in the community for many years, until his death in 1898. In keeping with the practice of introducing children into the economic life of the community, the boys of the Village, under Brother Samuel's direction, produced large quantities of pickles, for market as well as for family use. The work was conducted in the granite basement of the 1850 Boys' Shop, now part of the museum of Sabbathday Lake. The pickles were shipped in large barrels to the Portland firm of Edward D. Pettengill Co., which bottled and sold them under the "Shaker" brand name. Pettengill also distributed "Shaker" ketchup and horseradish, which was grated and prepared by the sisters of the community. The profitable business relationship between the Society and the Pettengill firm lasted for more than thirty years, until about the turn of the century.

In the twentieth century, the production of pickles, as well as fruit preserves, jams and jellies, became important among the sisters' trades, although perhaps not in the wholesale quantities of the prior century. In 1910, a guest at the Poland Spring House recorded her impressions of a visit to the Village:

It was preserving-time at the Sabbath Day Lake Settlement that day when we visited the Shakers. Fragrant puffs of boiling fruit and spices emanated from the basement kitchen and filled the halls; perhaps they were making the famous Shaker apple-sauce that day; the odors suggested it. We were told that the children were all below, helping to prepare fruit, but a sister, marvelling at a small, fluffy Chinese poodle which one of our party carried, suggested that "the children would greatly love to see the wonderful little dog." Consent being given, up trooped a dozen of the healthiest, rosiest-cheeked girls you ever saw, each attired from head to foot in an ample gingham apron. They arranged themselves decorously in a straight line on one side of the hall, and the poodle fortunately consented to do all his small stock of tricks for their amusement, to their evident delight. They were more quietly merry than our every-day noisy children would have been, and when the small entertainment was *over, at a word they went quietly back to their preserve-making.*

The Children's Orders

CHILDREN HAVE PLAYED an important and distinctive role in the United Society from the very early days of its history, when large families entered the community together. By all accounts, the life of Shaker children was very happy, although they were placed in Boys' and Girls' Orders under the supervision of their own brother and sister caretakers rather than continuing to live in the individual households that they had known.

This separation of husbands from wives and parents from children is often viewed as an unfortunate or negative practice of the Society; indeed, nineteenth-century opponents of the Shakers characterized it as a calculated effort to replace the natural ties of affection with an unimpeded loyalty to the church. Bitterness ensued, especially when one spouse was lukewarm or opposed to the Shaker testimony while the other embraced it without reserve. For the unbelieving husband or wife, such a decision on the part of a loved one could be heartbreaking. To their credit, the Shakers demanded that the believing partner come to a fair and equitable settlement with his or her spouse before entering the Society, and refused to admit those who had not, but rancor and acrimony sometimes resulted nevertheless.

After leaving the Shakers, Mary Dyer of New Hampshire and Eunice Chapman of New York, whose husbands and children remained among Believers, lived out their lives in desperate and bitter struggles against the Society, seeking the enactment of repressive legislation, pamphleteering, collecting names on petitions and affidavits, and instituting court proceedings. More often than not, the Shakers effectively defended their way of life against these and similar charges, presenting a very different picture of their communities from that offered by their op-

Shaker family at prayer in the dining room

ponents. Although there were occasional abuses by overzealous leaders, the record of the Society is remarkably clear. A petty tyranny could not last long in a free and democratic society. (It is a common misconception that the Shaker leadership governs absolutely. On the contrary, no rule or order is considered established in the Society without the "union" or mutual approbation of the membership, a principle recognized in the Shaker Church Covenant. Similarly, appointments to community office must be ratified by the members.)

It may be difficult for nonBelievers to understand, but husbands and wives making the voluntary choice to enter the Society to live as sisters and brothers have done so as a result of a profound conviction that God was calling them to another, and for them, more authentic kind of love. The Shakers find scriptural authority in the answer of Jesus to Peter (Mark 10:29–30)—

. . . There is no man that hath left house, or brethren, or sisters, or father, or mother, or wife, or children, or lands for my sake and the gospel's; but he shall receive an hundred fold now in this time, houses and brethren and sisters, and mothers and children, and lands, with persecution, and in the world to come, eternal life.

This is not to suggest that even for committed Believers there was not a trial to be faced in the new relationship, but the records of the Society make it clear that most adjusted to their chosen life. In 1862, Abner and Elmira Douglas entered the community at Sabbathday Lake as Believers, accompanied by their young daughters, Sirena and Mary Ella, and very soon were well integrated into the full and diverse life of late-nineteenth-century Shakerism in Maine. Although Abner and Elmira "always conducted themselves very properly toward each other," as Eldress Mary Ann Gillespie was later to observe, and "never made an hour's trouble, relative to their children," it is clear that the members of the Douglas family never wavered in their affection for each other.

Community memories retain many stories involving children. Here is one recorded by Sister Aurelia Mace in her commonplace book.

Israel Cushman and Elder Henry's Hat

Elder Henry Clough came from New Lebanon to minister to the people in Maine soon after the Societies were organized . . . Ruth Holmes, Oliver's sister, wanted to get the measure of Elder Henry's head, or hat, without his knowledge, for she wanted to surprise him with the present of a new hat. How did she get his hat to measure? Israel Cushman was then about 13 years of age. Ruth Holmes came to the front door of the old washhouse . . . She saw Israel in the dooryard and said to him, "Is there any way that you can get Elder Henry's hat for me for five minutes?" He answered, "I think so." He marched out into the orchard, boy fashion, went up to Elder Henry, reached, and took his hat off from his head, put it on his own head and put his hat on Elder Henry's head. Then he went to Ruth, she measured the hat—and he returned to the orchard and swapped them back again.—

It showed Elder Henry's kind and loving disposition that a boy could feel freedom to be so familiar with him.

If children were given responsibilities when they were able to accept them they were also allowed great latitude by their caretakers in exercising their young imaginations. In her "Notes about Home" for *The Manifesto* in June 1893, Sister Ada Cummings recorded how the little girls of the community held a memorial service for a deceased bird.

They found in the grass an oriole which for some cause had just departed this life, and tenderly laid it in a box; took it with their hands full of flowers, to the cemetery where they had a little funeral. Sung: "Hushed are the strivings of nature," and "I shall

know my own in heaven." Each made a little speech, then the leader said: "Would the Brethren and Sisters like to take a last look at the deceased?" At this time they were all weeping, and the bird was buried on Sr. Mary Ella's grave. Finally they strewed the flowers on that and a number of other graves and marched back to the house in a very solemn manner.

When Sister Aurelia visited with these children and their teacher, Sister Ada, later the same year, she found them planning to hold a Shaker meeting of their own. She taught them the "Celestial March" and other religious exercises "which made the worship of our fathers and mothers so beautiful." As she led the children in the dance, Aurelia stood between two worlds. She passed along a heritage that would enrich generations of Shakers yet to be, but was herself transported to the days of her own youth. It "caused me to think," she later wrote, "of the pure and holy lives our fathers and mothers lived."

MOTHER LUCY ON THE RESPONSIBILITY OF CARETAKERS

[The recorded sayings of Mother Lucy Wright, one of the Society's great early-nineteenth-century leaders, were compiled after her death in 1821. They continue to serve as private devotional reading for the Sabbathday Lake Shakers and are regularly read in meeting. This text includes her instructions to the brother and sister caretakers of the Boys' and Girls' Orders.]

Mother Lucy seemed to feel great anxiety for the children. She would often speak of the great responsibility their guardians were under to care for their daily welfare, their protection; the example before them, the language used to them; all this should be the burden of those who care for them. She would speak particularly to the children and youth, saying, "You are young; your youth is the best and easiest time for you to learn to serve God. I wish you could realize this. I pray for you often for I feel the burden of your salvation, and desire you to live a life of uprightness.

The Shakers practiced only the mildest form of discipline on the children in their care. Corporal punishment was not encouraged. In the 1820s, Sister Sarah Palmer was caretaker of the little girls. Once, when the children quarreled, Sister Sarah told them to kneel and say, "more love and unicorn." "That was her funny way," Sister Aurelia later recorded, "unicorn instead of union. That would cause them to smile and be pleasant."

OTIS SAWYER AND CREAM FISH AND POTATOES

Otis was dearly loved as a little boy.—When the Ministry would come up to Poland for a day's visit, the sisters would get them a special dinner, generally cream fish and potatoes. Little Otis said one day, "I wish I was one of the Ministry, so I could have cream fish and potatoes; Eldress Lucy [Prescott] heard of it, and after they were done she called Otis in, had him sit in her chair and have a nice dinner of cream fish and potatoes. He little thought then of the years that he would yet be in the Ministry—and have cream fish and potatoes.

As the nineteenth century progressed, more and more children were brought to the Shakers as orphans or children requiring the care their parents or guardians could not provide. Because of these and the other children entering the Society with their parents, the question of schooling became important. However, there is little recorded information available about education in the earliest years of the community's history. In 1823, Brother Seth Youngs Wells came to New Gloucester and Poland Hill from the parent community at New Lebanon as part of a tour of the various societies to establish and standardize Shaker education. As was his practice in each community, he taught a brief term of school himself and trained a promising candidate to serve as

teacher after he left the community. After Brother Seth's departure, the thirty-one year old John Coffin took charge of the school and held classes for the Shaker children at Sabbathday Lake for many years. Other dedicated teachers followed, perhaps none with a more distinguished record than Sister Aurelia Mace, who taught for twenty-five years beginning in 1856.

Although we now associate the autumn season with the beginning of the school year, it was not always so among the Maine Shakers. Because of the requirements of community industry, a winter term was held for boys—when there was less farm work to be done—and a summer term for girls. In the last quarter of the nineteenth century, boys and girls began to be schooled together, the long term beginning in November.

Until 1880, there was no special school building in the community. But at a meeting of the Town of New Gloucester, which several of the Shaker brethren attended, the members voted to appropriate $750 for the building of a schoolhouse in the Shaker Village to serve not only the Shaker children but all those who resided in School District No. 9, as the western part of the town was designated. The building was designed by Brother Hewitt Chandler, the Society contributing $300 to its cost in addition to a total of $800 that the town eventually provided. It was located immediately north of the Ministry's Shop and continued to serve as a schoolhouse until the remaining rural school districts were consolidated in 1950.

The closing of the old one-room schoolhouse placed a great burden on the children of the Society. Previously, the sons and daughters of the Shakers' neighbors came into the Village to be taught, where the Shaker children felt secure and at home. But after 1950, Shaker children were required to attend classes outside of the Village and sometimes felt pitied by their classmates. One little girl, a resident of the Village in the 1950s and early 1960s, believed that the other children placed the young Shakers on a pedestal. It was somehow necessary to live up to their preconceived expectations of how a Shaker should act. At least one sister in the 1950s thought the situation unhealthy for the children.

Shaker schoolhouse

"They were sent to us," she said, "but it really isn't good for them. Now we don't have our own school, and they have to attend the public schools; and it's hard on them . . ."

Although young life would return to the Village again in the 1970s, the children's orders at Sabbathday Lake were closed out in the early 1960s. The schoolhouse was sold to a neighboring farmer and moved down the road just south of the Village to be used for apple and grain storage, where eventually it fell into disrepair. But after many years of neglect, it is returning to the Village. Concerned for the preservation of this important symbol of their heritage, the Sabbathday Lake Shakers, with the assistance of friends and supporters, have purchased the building. It will be placed on its original foundation and a fireproof vault, constructed to look like the now missing school woodshed, will be added to house the Society's Shaker Library.

Library and Institute

THE SHAKER LIBRARY, as now constituted, had its beginnings in 1883, when Elder Otis Sawyer arranged for Elder Henry Green of Alfred, a talented cabinetmaker, to construct a bookcase in which every publication of the United Society was to be shelved. For his efforts, Elder Henry charged $25, including delivery. His original bookcase remains in the library today, although others have joined it.

The initial collection of books assembled by Elder Otis contained one hundred seventy-five volumes, but that represented only a fraction of the Society's total publishing effort. Beginning with Father Joseph Meacham's *Concise Statement* in 1790, the several communities of Shakers have published hundreds of books and pamphlets, including histories, theological studies, hymnbooks, biographies and autobiographies, ethical works, catalogues, advertising brochures and leaflets, treatises on a variety of subjects from farming to music, poetry, texts received by inspiration during the Era of Mother's Work, monthly and quarterly journals and a host of others. Total volumes in the Shaker Library, which includes non-Shaker works about the Shakers, now amount to over 15,000 not including the library's vast archival, photographic and manuscript holdings. These handwritten journals, records, books of account, legal instruments, diaries, letters, songbooks and other manuscripts, which represent a unique resource on the history of the Maine Shakers and the United Society as a whole, are of inestimable value. They also often demonstrate a consummate skill with the pen. Particularly lovely are the manuscript hymnals, which contain the Shaker letteral notation, and the "gift" messages, believed to have been received by inspiration. These are examples of the calligrapher's art at its best.

Beginning each autumn, at the start of the academic year, scores of students and researchers at all levels arrive in the Village to use the library's resources. During the last decade or two, as a result of Brother Theodore Johnson's leadership, education has become a major thrust of the community's life. The Shaker Library is located in the Central Brick Dwelling. It now occupies three rooms in the house, including a pleasant reading room at the southeast corner of the first floor. More often than not, one or more researchers from the world will be found there, poring over the old records. (Occasionally, they will be pleasantly surprised by Sister Frances inviting them down to the kitchen for tea and cookies.) Under the direction of Brother Ted, the library has been professionally organized and catalogued, containing many of the amenities expected in a modern research facility, including microfilm readers. But even with all its new conveniences, it is the fact that the library is located in that great old dwellinghouse, with its sweet

scent of apples and its compelling associations with the Shaker way in Maine, that makes research there a special delight.

Several years ago, Brother Theodore established the Institute for Shaker Studies at the Village to further the community's educational goals. Each year the institute organizes classes, lectures and workshops on various aspects of the Shaker tradition in areas as diverse as theology and spinning, dyeing and weaving. It has sponsored joint courses of study with the University of Southern Maine and has participated in several programs funded by the Maine State Council on the Arts and Humanities, including a continuing program for high school students at the nearby Gray-New Gloucester High School. These programs are staffed by community members and outsiders with established credentials. As an adjunct to the Shaker Library, which is composed only of works bearing directly on the history, faith, arts and economic life of Believers, the institute maintains a large library in the Central Brick Dwelling that provides the broader context for Shaker studies. This library houses several specialized collections on such subjects as the Freewill Baptists (with whom the Shakers competed for souls in the ferment of frontier revivalism two hundred years ago) and the cultivation, gathering and medicinal uses of herbs, among others. Brothers Theodore and Arnold devote considerable energy to institute projects not only during the autumn season, but throughout the rest of the year as well.

The establishment of the Institute for Shaker Studies has resulted in a continuing and creative dialogue between the Believers and members of the academic community, which in turn has fostered the development of serious inquiry by professional theologians, historians and sociologists into the life and faith of the United Society. The presence of these scholars in the Village has provided the community with encouragement, in that its educational goals are being realized.

In furtherance of these objectives, the Shaker Society at Sabbathday Lake has renewed its publishing activities, and several distinguished works have appeared under its imprint in the 1970s and 1980s. In 1983, for example, the Society published *Gift Drawing and Gift Song: A Study of Two Forms of Shaker Inspiration*, by Professor Daniel W. Patterson of the University of North Carolina at Chapel Hill. It has also published several important but smaller works by members of the community, among them informative histories of the Alfred and Sabbathday Lake communities by Sister Mildred, and eloquent considerations of Shaker religious faith and creativity by Brother Theodore. *Shaker Your Plate: Of Shaker Cooks and Cooking*, Sister Frances' excellent cookbook, was published by the Society in 1985.

Throughout the years, many in the Society have spoken eloquently in public forums on the Shaker faith, including Sister Aurelia Mace.

SISTER AURELIA ON GOD THE MOTHER

In 1904, Sister Aurelia delivered a lecture at Greenacre in Eliot, Maine. Entitled "The Mission and Testimony of the Shakers of the Twentieth Century to the World," it emphasized the continued relevance of Shaker ideas. Her reference to the Motherhood of God, long accepted in Shakerism, has a curious late twentieth century ring to it. "God, our infinite Mother," she said, "created the beautiful things, the flowers and the singing birds, music and the visions which flow into the soul of a poet. She is forever drawing us nearer and nearer unto her beautiful Self, the source of elegance and refinement. She is leading me beside the still waters."

Sister Aurelia presented readings from her book, *The Aletheia: Spirit of Truth*, a collection of topical essays and poetry on Shaker life, to audiences at the Poland Spring House and elsewhere.

Although the Sabbathday Lake Shakers were not as active in printing or publishing earlier in their history, they have an interesting and little known tradition in these pursuits. In 1847, Deacon James Holmes of New Gloucester printed a new edition of Father Joseph Meacham's *Concise Statement*, and in the 1850s followed that effort by compiling and printing a series of three books containing hints for farmers. In the preface to one of these "farmer's books," Deacon James,

who had entered the Society as a child with his parents in 1783 in the first opening of the gospel at Thompson's Pond Plantation, included a statement that is at once a testimony to his humility and his ingenuity. "The publisher, " he wrote, "an octogenarian

who has neither press nor fixtures for printing, the types excepted, but those of his own invention, *begs leave to say, that, if the reader detects errors, either in typography or in mechanical execution, he hopes the above assertion may be received as sufficient apology . . .*

Deacon James also printed a collection of anthems "given by the spirits" in the period from 1837 to 1848, during the height of the Era of Manifestations.

The Shaker Society published a monthly journal from 1871 through 1899 under several titles: *The Shaker* (1871–1872, 1876–1877); *Shaker and Shakeress* (1873–1875); *The Shaker Manifesto* (1872–1882); and *The Manifesto* (1883–1899). After *The Manifesto* was discontinued in 1899, Eldress Josephine Wilson presented the printing press at Canterbury, New Hampshire (where the monthly had been printed after 1886) to the Sabbathday Lake Shakers. It was used earlier this century by Brother Earl Campbell to print a number of booklets by members of the community, including Sister Jennie Mathers' compilations of Shaker recipes and poetry. From 1961 through 1974, the Society at Sabbathday Lake published a quarterly journal, *The Shaker Quarterly*, edited by Brother Theodore, that contained a rich assortment of material on all facets of Shaker life and lore.

Other Fall Activities

AUTUMN IS THE time for state and county fairs in New England. Their separation from the world has not prevented the Shakers from participating in these yearly events. Indeed, earlier in this century, the corn, beans and potatoes that Sister Eva Libby chose from the bounty of the season to enter into county fair competitions, often won ribbons for her and the Society.

Brother Delmer Wilson was especially proud of the huge squashes that came from his garden. One, weighing 154 pounds, filled an entire wheelbarrow. Sometimes large groups of Believers attended the fairs for the sheer enjoyment of it, as when twenty-eight members of the Alfred Society accepted the invitation of the president of the Portland and Rochester Railroad for a free ride to Portland and the New England Fair grounds. State and county fairs were also excellent places for the sisters to sell their fancywork.

For the last several years, Brother Arnold Hadd and Sister Marie Burgess have represented the Society at the important Eastern States Exposition in Springfield, Massachusetts, which is Brother Arnold's hometown. There they set up a table of their wares, including Shaker culinary herbs and herbal teas, jellies and jams, and sewn and knit products, as well as publications and recordings. The Believers also participate each fall in the Common Ground Country Fair of the Maine Organic Farmers and Gardeners Association at Windsor, Maine.

In a community that must schedule its work according to the immutable rhythms of nature's clock, drying and packing the year's gathering of herbs is an important autumn activity. Although the Village retains its 1824 Herb House, the building is in need of interior repair, and herb drying and packing are now undertaken at the Laundry or Sisters' Shop, a community building that has always served a variety of purposes. In the attic of the building, where clothes were once hung to dry on moveable racks, herbs are now dried. The blending of their pungent and pleasing aromas is apparent even as you approach the room. After sufficient time has elapsed and the drying process is completed, the herbs are brought to the spacious Ironing Room, where a wood-burning stove for heating the old-fashioned irons indicates the original purpose of the room. Here the Shakers cut or chop and crumble the various herbs and roots, weigh them carefully, and pack them in Society's well-known tins, the labels for which are printed by Brother Arnold. It is a time-consuming process, in which

many members of the community and often some young friends participate. In addition to shop sales, the Shakers maintain a vigorous wholesale and mail-order business in packaged herbs, and the tins must be ready for shipment as needed.

All this activity takes place in the Laundry, one of the Village's most interesting structures. It was originally built in 1821 and then completely remodeled by Brother Hewitt Chandler in 1878. Although intended for many purposes, the Laundry or Sisters' Shop receives its name from the spacious laundry room on its ground floor.

At one end of the room is a huge old Shaker washing machine, one of the inventions for which nineteenth-century Believers were famous. Early in that century, the Shakers of New Lebanon, New York, purchased the rights to a newly patented washing machine and began experimenting with it. On January 26, 1858, Brother Nicholas Bennett of the New Lebanon Society received a United States patent for an Improved Washing Machine, which he transferred to David Parker, trustee of the Canterbury Society, where the machine was to be manufactured for sale to the world. Brother Nicholas divided a large tub into several compartments, each of which operated independently of the other, so that separate washing operations could take place simultaneously. The machine, which was operated by a steam engine, could handle large-scale operations and was sold by the Shakers to hotels, hospitals and other institutions well into the nineteenth century. In 1876, they exhibited the machine at the Centennial Exposition at Philadelphia, where it received the Gold Medal, and in 1877, two brethren at Canterbury received a United States patent for additional improvements to the machine. Although one of these old machines, which still may be seen in the Laundry at Sabbathday Lake, remains in operating condition, the family now uses a smaller, modern washing machine located in the same room.

Although the Laundry received its name from the operations on its ground floor, other activities, such as weaving and tailoring, were carried

on there as well. A series of individual sewing rooms, still in active use by the sisters, are also located in the building. In one of these rooms, Sister Elsie has turned out hundreds of aprons and other articles for sale in the Shaker store, while Sister Minnie works at the well-known round potholders for which she is famous. Each sister has a beautiful late-nineteenth-century Shaker sewing desk in contrasting pine and birch, with red and natural stains. In the tailoring room, there is a large press on which another Shaker innovation was produced for many years during the nineteenth century, a waterproof, permanent press fabric, perhaps the first in the nation. In their sewing rooms, the sisters also work at refurbishing and replacing the linings and interiors of old Shaker sewing "carriers" brought to them by collectors.

Several members of the community remain skilled in the practice of taping or "listing" the seats of chairs, too, and occasionally may be found placing a new seat on one of the Society's innumerable Shaker chairs or rockers, or providing this service for a member of the public. Here are instructions for taping the seat of a chair or rocker.

Brother Arnold seating or "listing" a Shaker chair

"Listing" or "Taping" a Shaker Chair

Brightly colored woven tape seats in checkerboard or herringbone designs have long been associated with Shaker chairs. These instructions are based on the method used by Sister Elsie A. McCool.

MATERIALS:

1. "Shaker" tape. This is now produced by several manufacturers in a variety of colors and may be purchased from the Sabbathday Lake Shakers or other suppliers. If you specify the size of your chair seat, the supplier will determine the correct amount of tape required.

2. Quilted or padded fabric of any kind in the size of the chair seat plus six inches all around.

3. Needle and heavy thread.

4. Upholsterer's tacks.

INSTRUCTIONS:

1. Cut padded or quilted fabric as indicated in Figure A. Fold the four "flaps" under the seat and, using needle and heavy thread, sew flaps to upper part of fabric, creating an "underseat."

2. Start taping by securing one end of tape to the left back rung of the chair, using two upholsterer's tacks. See Figure B.

3. Wrap tape around the front rung of the chair, drawing it under the quilted or padded fabric and back around the rear rung. Continue wrapping in this manner, each row directly next to the other and perpendicular to the front and back rungs. Upon reaching the right back post, tack the tape to the inside of the rung, as you did at the start. Cut off any remaining tape. Because of the splayed shape of most seats there will be two triangular spaces without tape on either side, as indicated in Figure C.

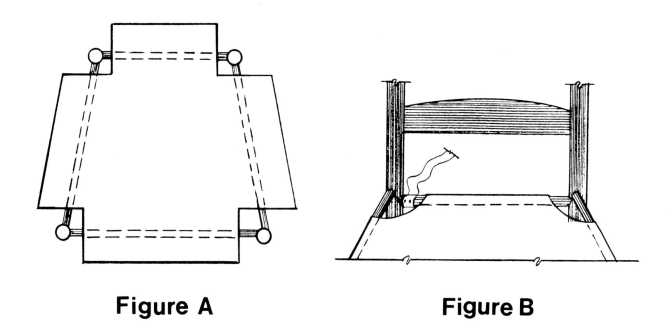

Figure A   **Figure B**

4. To fill in the triangular spaces, use separate lengths of cut tape, each just long enough to form a single row above and below the seat. Begin this step from the inside (i.e., immediately next to the first row of tape you wrapped around the seat) and work, row by row, from there. Each length of tape will be smaller than the previous one, as you move toward the side of the chair and the remaining triangular space is reduced in size. Affix each of these separate lengths to the inside side rung of the seat, using upholsterer's tacks, wrapping each around and under the front rung and back to where you started. Repeat this process with the other triangular shape, again working from the inside.

5. You are now ready to begin weaving. To start, secure the end of the tape on the left side rung at back of the chair with an upholsterer's tack (similar to Figure A).

6. To do a checkerboard pattern, as illustrated in Figure D, weave "under one over one" from left to right. (A contrasting color is traditional and creates a lovely effect.) Turn the chair over and repeat the weave on the underside. Continue this process, one row next to the others, above and below the seat, until reaching the front posts and then secure tape with upholsterer's tacks to the underside of the rung. Cut off any excess tape.

Other activities are also associated with autumn and the gathering of its harvests. For many years in the late eighteenth and much of the nineteenth century, the Shakers operated a gristmill to which farmers in the area would bring their wheat, rye, corn and other grains for milling. Earlier gristmills, constructed in 1786 and 1809, were replaced by the 1853 Great Mill, which, as we have seen, also had facilities for

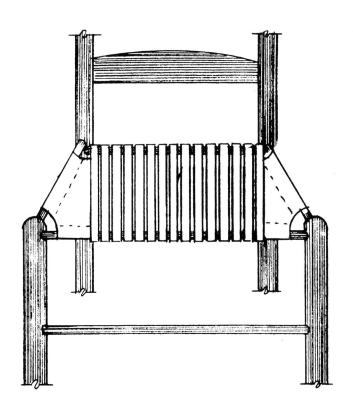

Figure C

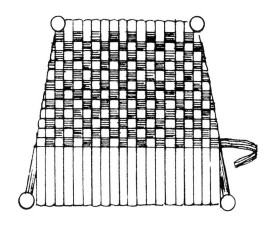

Figure D

carding wool and sawing. The sisters' trades always have been active in the fall, as well. One old-fashioned practice was the production of fir balsam pillows, a trade that was under the direction of Sister Aurelia from 1870 to until the time of her death in 1910. Thousands of pillows were sold during that period; they remain available in more limited quantities to this day.

Symbols of gathering may be seen in the hundreds of baskets, wooden "carriers," and oval boxes that remain in the community. Evidencing the excellence in workmanship associated with Shaker craftsmanship, many of these beautiful objects continue to be used, although others have been chosen for museum exhibition. The oval box is so ubiquitous that it appears emblematic of Shaker life. Brother Delmer Wilson continued to make oval boxes and carriers almost until his death in 1961.

While they attend to the various chores of fall, the gathering of the last fruits of the season, the cutting of ensilage, and the chopping of wood for later use in winter stoves, the Sabbathday Lake Shakers remain mindful of the splendor around them. On a lovely October day in 1894, Sister Ada Cummings, Village schoolmistress and poet, lingered for a moment on a stroll along the wooded shores of the lake. As she considered the autumn magnificence, an "unbidden thought" pressed itself onto her consciousness: "how soon the beauty fades away."

These autumn days are warning us
Of winter sure to be,
When all the leaves have fallen off
From every branch and tree.

These earthly friends are leaving us
Their autumns being past;
And thus the winters of our lives
Will come to us at last.

Making a Shaker Carrier

Through much of their history, the Shakers produced oval boxes in a seemingly endless number of sizes. These well-proportioned, delicate but sturdy containers, with their characteristic "fingers" or "swallow-tails," were used for storage in dwellinghouses and shops. Displayed in stacks of graduated sizes, they are prized by today's collectors. Elder Delmer Wilson made thousands of oval boxes during his long Shaker life. Many of these, fitted with "bales" or handles, are known as "carriers." In one of his more productive seasons, Elder Delmer made 1,083 carriers. The carrier described here is based on one of his.

MATERIALS:
1. Clear pine approximately 6" x 8" (or sufficiently large to allow you to cut out an ellipse as shown in top view) and planed to ¼" in thickness for the bottom of the carrier
2. A strip of maple 2½" x 24" for the side of the carrier
3. A strip of maple ½" x 14" for the handle
4. Twenty ½" copper tacks
5. Two ⅛" rivets
6. Six ¼" copper washers

CONSTRUCTION:
1. Before beginning, try to study an original Shaker oval box or carrier in a museum or private collection. You will acquire a better understanding of the balance and proportions of the box by careful observation of an original. Patience is a Shaker virtue!
2. To make the bottom, accurately measure an ellipse on the pine board, in the dimensions shown in the top view, and cut out carefully with a jig, saber or coping saw. Sand all sides and edges until they are smooth.
3. For the side of the carrier, hand plane and sand the maple strip evenly so that it is ³⁄₃₂" thick. Then draw "fingers" as shown in front view, 2" long. Cut with a sharp modeling or razor knife. Then, using sandpaper, taper the end opposite the fingers.

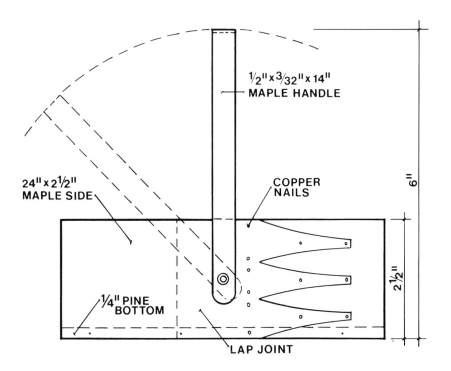

½" x 3/32" x 14"
MAPLE HANDLE

COPPER
NAILS

24" x 2½"
MAPLE SIDE

¼" PINE
BOTTOM

LAP JOINT

6"

2½"

FRONT VIEW

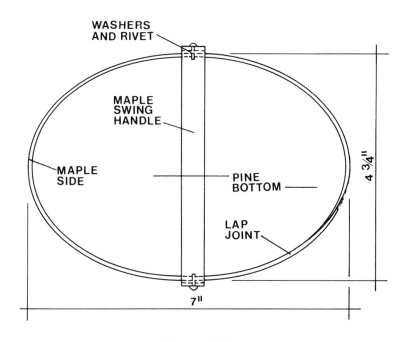

WASHERS
AND RIVET

MAPLE
SWING
HANDLE

MAPLE
SIDE

PINE
BOTTOM

LAP
JOINT

4 ¾"

7"

TOP VIEW

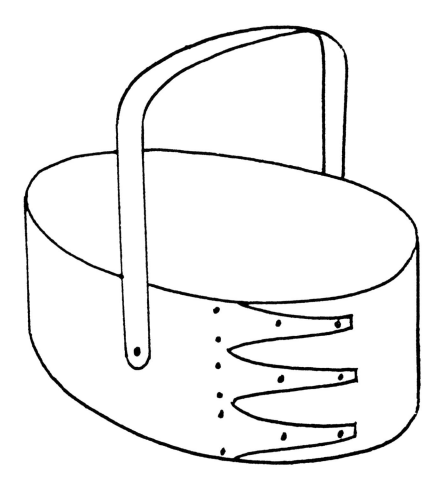

4. The placement of tacks is traditional and characteristic of Shaker oval boxes and carriers. In order to avoid splitting, pre-drill holes for the tacks, *eight* along the base to attach pine bottom, and *twelve* in three vertical rows adjacent to and on the fingers, as shown in front view.

5. Soak entire maple side in hot water until sufficiently pliable to wrap around the base without splitting. After applying a small amount of glue along the edge of the base, carefully wrap the maple side around the base, tacking it together as you progress. After the base is secured, the fingers should be tacked as well. A small amount of glue placed under the fingers will be helpful in this process. Let dry thoroughly and sand as necessary.

6. For the handle, round the ends as shown in front view. Hand plane and sand to a thickness of $3/32''$. Then pre-drill a hole at each end through which the rivet will be driven, and soak in hot water for ten minutes or until pliable. Bend handle to a U-shape as shown in the drawing of the completed carrier.

7. Drill a hole in each side of the carrier $1\frac{1}{4}''$ from the bottom, as shown in front view, and affix handle using rivets and washers.

8. After drying, apply a maple stain, lacquer and polish.

Shaker Mourning Customs

FOR A PEOPLE accepting the idea of a continuing life in the spirit, death is perceived as "harvest time." We have seen that committed Believers live in daily awareness of the closeness of the spiritual world and the mediating presence of departed saints and the hosts of heaven. For the Shakers, the life process as we know it is a representation of an unfolding spiritual reality, "the material and spiritual having their seasons of sowing and harvesting," as Eldress Fannie Casey of the church at Alfred expressed it in 1895. Much of the literature of the church, its songs and its lore, reflects this idea.

Shaker funerals are solemn events, but there is a sense of joyous fulfillment in the service as well. Although the "set songs" appointed for the occasion are ones traditionally used in funerals, and there is an emphasis on the life and witness of the deceased in the personal testimonies of the assembled members of the family, the meeting itself remains open to the moving of the spirit and is not unlike other Shaker services of worship. In the nineteenth century, it was not unusual for the spirit of the departed to be manifest at the funeral and to bring a blessing upon those present.

At Sabbathday Lake, memorial services are held in the family chapel of the Central Brick Dwelling. Burial follows in a little graveyard just

Let My Name Be Recorded

GLOUCESTER, ME.

Let my name be re - cord - ed In the book the an - gels keep, Where each

act is re-ward - ed, And the seed I have sown I shall reap.

So when the an - gel reap -er cometh, And the harvest time shall be,

I shall find in my Father's house, There's a mansion reserved for me.

Let my name be recorded
In the book the angels keep,
Where each act is rewarded,
And the seed I have sown I shall reap.

So when the angel reaper cometh,
And the harvest time shall be,
I shall find in my Father's house,
There's a mansion reserved for me.

Church Family cemetery, Sabbathday Lake,
Maine

to the north of the Village. Although separate, simple gravestones once marked the resting place of the Believers, there is but a single central monument in the cemetery, with one engraved word—SHAKERS. The Society maintains a complete register of the Believers who have been interred there, with the precise place of their burial, but the graveyard itself is a green expanse of shaded lawn in which the faithful departed of the church rest in communal anonymity.

Thanksgiving

FOR THE SHAKERS, as for all Americans, Thanksgiving is the major civil holiday of the fall season. At Shaker Village, the celebration of the day is centered in the ground floor of the brick dwellinghouse, where the principal kitchen and dining room of the community are located. In fact, the very first meal shared by the Sabbathday Lake Shakers in their new dwelling, after its completion in 1884, was on Thanksgiving. Before they gather for the day's feast, the Shakers meet at 10:00 in the family chapel of the dwellinghouse for a worship service. The theme of the meeting inevitably is one of gratitude.

THANKSGIVING DAY, 1970

November 26 was indeed a day of Thanksgiving. We do not need a special day on which to count our blessings or to give thanks to the maker of all. Thankfulness is not a transient experience, but an overflowing love of God which fills the whole being with constant humble recognition of His goodness and great gifts to us. It is an experience that knows no day or time, but is as constant as our breathing and fills our whole being. This spirit alone produces the acceptable worship of God which awakens within us continually a thankful response to Him and His work. As we shared our sumptuous meal with friends . . . I was reminded of our first Gospel parents whose meals were often a crust of bread with tears of thankfulness running down their cheeks.

Sister R. Mildred Barker

In the large kitchen of the brick dwelling-house with its modern ten-burner range and old-fashioned arch kettle, heated by a wood-burning stove, almost side by side, Sister Frances Carr and her assistants are busy from the early hours of Thanksgiving morning preparing the holiday feast. The main course, turkey with sage dressing, is a longtime community favorite.

Sister Frances' Turkey with Bread Stuffing

2 pounds white bread, broken into small pieces
2 cups hot water
1 cup butter or margarine, melted
2 cups chopped onion
2 eggs, beaten lightly
2 tablespoons Shaker sage, crushed
Salt and pepper to taste

Pour water and melted butter over bread. Allow bread to soften. Sauté onions over low heat until just tender; do not overcook. Add eggs, onion and seasonings to bread. Mix thoroughly. Taste, or better still have others around you taste, as it makes it interesting to add whatever bit of seasonings others may like. In addition to the sage I like to add approximately 1 teaspoon of Bell's Seasoning.

Thoroughly wash bird. Dry interior with paper towel. Thoroughly rub interior with mixture of butter and sage. Rub all over bird, giving special heed to wing areas. Roast at 300 degrees for the recommended time for the bird.

Before sitting down to the noon dinner, the Shakers sing a traditional Thanksgiving song:

All at Home

What shall be the theme of the passing hour?
What shall be the measure of the song, what the strain?
Once more the circle's made wider and broader,
The household of faith have all met again.

Come, the feast is ready
While the table's loaded
With the choicest fruit from afar and near,
While leaders and people, parents and children,
Love and affection, all are here.

All at home. All at home.

Gathered together at Thanksgiving, the Believers look back to a sacred heritage. The four seasons of their year, and of their life, comprise a rich, diverse and wonderful legacy not only for them, but for the world as well. Even at a time of introspection like Thanksgiving, however, the Sabbathday Lake Shakers continue to look forward.

Brothers Ted and Arnold at prayers

ALL THINGS ANEW

The light kindled in that first meeting in Gowen Wilson's farmhouse has not yet been extinguished. We pray God that it may never be. Although it may not seem to burn as brightly as it once did, it is still alive. It has the latent power to kindle within human hearts the warmth of divine love and peace. It has the power to bring light into the minds of all those seekers who are open to divine truth and understanding.

Although few in number, it is our resolution that we be caught up more and more in the blessed work of God. We pray that with heavenly Guidance we may so make ourselves instruments of divine truth and light that the way of Believers may once again appear to the children of God as a meaningful, vital and challenging way of life.

The Sabbathday Lake Shakers

Other Seasons, Other Years: An Afterword

Near the end of the nineteenth century, Sister Aurelia Mace recorded her observations about the state of the community. "The present condition of the Society," she wrote, "is more highly Spiritual than I have ever known it to be before."

Even at the time of the Manifestations there was not that understanding of the beauty and pleasantness of the straight and narrow way. Nor that determination in the younger class to keep their feet in that way.

As Sister Aurelia wrote these hopeful words, however, the very fabric of Shakerism seemed to be disintegrating elsewhere. Faced with decreasing numbers, especially among the brethren, and diminishing resources, the United Society was forced to close one village after another and to move surviving members to communities with better immediate prospects for continuity. The decision to discontinue *The Manifesto*, the Society's monthly publication, with the issue of December 1899, left the communities without a forum for the consideration of matters affecting their future or a means of communicating with each other. But as the process of retrenchment took its toll elsewhere, a full and robust Shakerism continued at Alfred and Sabbathday Lake.

To be sure, the Maine Shakers were also grappling with the problem of survival as they approached the new century. The Poland Hill family's closing and consolidation with the Church at Sabbathday Lake in 1887 meant that Maine was not immune to the problems affecting the Society as a whole, and the death late in the nineteenth century of leaders who had dominated Shaker life in the bishopric for many de-

cades signaled the need for a renewal of commitment in the younger generation. "As the ancients of the city pass away, who will keep the testimony burning bright?" asked a late Shaker hymn from Mount Lebanon. Fortunately for the continuity of the tradition, there were Shakers in Maine who were willing to accept the challenge.

Before the turn of the century, Eldress Fannie Casey of Alfred issued a call for Believers "to awaken and come forth and proclaim the mercy and goodness of God." She reminded them of Father James Whittaker's warning that "where the testimony was permitted to die out, there the life and power of the gospel would die out also." Against those within the Society who suggested that the principles of the movement would survive the closing out of the communities, Eldress Fannie held that there could be no Shakerism without Shakers. "May this never be the case with us," she prayed. Eldress Fannie's resolve was seconded by Sister Aurelia, who embraced the twentieth century on behalf of her church. Her stirring address, "The Mission and Testimony of the Shakers of the Twentieth Century to the World," delivered in the summer of 1904 to an audience at Eliot, Maine, offered the simple faith of Mother Ann to the world anew, a faith that she confidently saw descending "[f]rom above the magnificence of the landscape in a beautiful morning, and the sublimity of the rolling waves of the ocean; from above the grandeur of the rising and setting sun, and all the glories this world can bestow."

But what would the shape of twentieth-century Shakerism be? The same year that Sister Aurelia spoke at Eliot, Eldress Anna White and Sister Leila S. Taylor of Mount Lebanon argued that mere custom did not define the life or faith of the Church. "The Shaker may change his style of coat, may alter the cut of her gown or cease to wear a cap," they suggested, "and no harm be done. Vital harm may be done by retaining either . . . merely to preserve old forms and customs, when the time is crying out in vain for action." For thoughtful Shakers standing on the threshold of the new century, the principle of separation from the world, while still valid and necessary, no longer implied an insularity that might limit the opportunities for full intellectual growth, a factor in nineteenth-century Shakerism that had caused at least some gifted Believers (Brother Hewitt Chandler, among them) to turn their backs on the Society. Indeed, Sister Aurelia looked forward to the day when "all that is pure and elevating in art and the sciences" would be known in the Society.

The hope and determination with which the Maine Shakers entered the new century sustained them through its first fifty years, and the consolidation of the Alfred and New Gloucester communities in 1931 brought renewed strength to the bishopric. By mid-century, however, even the most resolute Believers at Sabbathday Lake began to be concerned that the inexorable disintegration that had plagued other communities would also visit them. Mount Lebanon, for 160 years the United Society's "center of union," closed its doors in 1947, leaving only Hancock, Massachusetts, with a handful of elderly members (Hancock itself closed in 1960), and Canterbury, New Hampshire, whose leaders had decided against the acceptance of new members. At Sabbathday Lake, a family consisting of a single brother, Elder Delmer C. Wilson, and perhaps two dozen sisters and some young girls did not seem to be the basis for a stable future. By remaining faithful, however, the little band created conditions that would ensure surprising vitality in the 1970s and 1980s.

The decision of Sister Frances A. Carr to accept the yoke of the Shaker faith as a young woman in 1948, after spending much of her childhood in the Village, and the entry of Brother Theodore E. Johnson into the full life of the family just over ten years later, signaled important new beginnings for the Sabbathday Lake Shakers. Indeed, the fact that Brother Ted, a Fulbright Scholar with a graduate degree in theology from Harvard University, was drawn to their life was seen as especially significant by the members of the community. Other young Believers, Brothers Arnold and Wayne among them, have followed.

The speech of the Sabbathday Lake Shakers is still laced with the simple "yea" and "nay" that has always characterized the conversation of Believers (a practice that is surprisingly natural and unselfconscious: visitors frequently fall into this usage soon after their introduction to the Village), and there is a comfortable familiarity and acceptance of the traditional ways of the faith. If much remains the same, much has changed. Only ruins now stand where the 1853 Great Mill once provided a means for community livelihood, but the family still benefits from the considerable timber reserves on its lands. As we have seen, the herb department and other pursuits provide part of the family's income; the Shakers also receive a modest income from investments and allocations from a trust established with funds from the sale of former Shaker properties. But their life through all the seasons of the year is still one of service and commitment and plenty of old-fashioned hard work.

The religious testimony of the Church is no longer withdrawn from the world. Through an active program of community outreach, the Sabbathday Lake Shakers regularly conduct worship services in various parts of the country. Sisters Mildred and Frances and Brothers Ted and Arnold also lecture widely. The family has also established close relations with other Christian and non-Christian religious communities. The exchange has resulted in mutual benefits. The liturgical practices, for example, of the well-known Benedictine community at Weston, Vermont, have been influenced by the monks' visits to Sabbathday Lake, and the Shakers are able again to experience a sense of belonging to a wider fellowship.

In September, 1874, the Sabbathday Lake Shakers participated in the centennial celebrations of the town of New Gloucester. Under a tent, 150 feet long by 65 feet wide, thirty-two members of the Society joined with their fellow citizens to mark the occasion. The Shakers provided home-baked breads, applesauce, "lots of cookies," melons and apples, pies, sweet cakes and other goodies. In introducing Elder Otis Sawyer, who was to address the assembled townsfolk, the chairman of the event offered a toast. "The United Society of Shakers," he said. "May their numbers never be less." It is a toast worth renewing now, at the end of another century.

My home, my sweet home in Zion,
My call, my holy call, how precious to me.
All the wealth this earth affords,
All the pleasures this vain world can give,
Never can purchase this treasure that I hold.
Although through deep waters and perils I pass,
Although with false brethren my lot may be cast,
Faith in God is my anchor and truth is my shield.
On these I rely when all else doth fail.

Otis Sawyer, 1855

Notes

A CHOSEN LIFE

ANNAH KENDALL'S REMINISCENCE OF
Mother Ann and the apple tree (p. 16) is
preserved in *Testimonies of the Life Character, Revelations and Doctrines of Mother Ann Lee, and the Elders with Her*, Rufus Bishop and Seth Youngs Wells, eds., Second Edition edited by Giles B. Avery (Albany, New York: Weed, Parsons & Co., 1888), p. 259. The story of Sabbathday Lake and the origin of its name (p. 16) may be found in Daphne Winslow Merrill, *The Lakes of Maine: A Compilation of Facts and Legend* (Rockland, Maine: Courier-Gazette, Inc., 1973), p. 145. Charles Edson Robinson, *A Concise History of the United Society of Believers Called Shakers* (East Canterbury, New Hampshire: Shaker Society, 1893), p. 97, describes the changing designation of the village and its post office (p. 17). See also Sister Eleanor Philbrook's brief but engaging "A Brief History of the Shaker Post Office, Sabbathday Lake, Maine," *The Shaker Quarterly* 4 (Spring 1964, pp. 38-40). The description of early Shaker worship (pp. 23-24) is quoted from Calvin Green and Seth Youngs Wells, *A Summary View of the Millennial Church, or United Society of Believers* (Albany, New York: Packard & van Benthuysen, 1823), p. 5. Ann Lee's reflections on her husband (p. 25) is preserved by Rufus Bishop and Seth Youngs Wells in their important compilation of church traditions, *Testimonies of the Life, Character, Revelations and Doctrines of Our Ever Blessed Mother Ann Lee, and the Elders with Her* (Hancock, Massachusetts: J. Tallcott and J. Deming, Jrs., 1816), p. 45. This work also is the source for the early characterization of the mission of Mother Ann, quoted on p. 25. *The Constables' Accounts of the Manor of Manchester*, edited by J.P. Earwaker (Manchester: H. Blacklock and Co., 1892) provides essential information about the Shakers' confrontation with English justice. The quote on p. 26 may be found on p. 256 of vol. 3 of this work. Green and Wells, *A Summary View* . . . is the source of the material quoted on

p. 26. The reaction of the Freewill Baptists to Shaker inroads into their congregations (p. 34) is reported in I.D. Stewart, *The History of the Freewill Baptists* (Dover, New Hampshire: Freewill Baptist Printing Establishment, 1862), p. 69. For a fascinating account of religion on the frontier, see Stephen A. Marini, *Radical Sects of Revolutionary New England* (Cambridge: Harvard University Press, 1982). Elder Otis Sawyer's description of the first Shaker meeting at Gowen Wilson's farm (p. 34) is contained in an address he delivered to the town meeting celebrating the centennial of New Gloucester. It is quoted in T.H. Haskell, ed., *The New Gloucester Centennial* (Portland, Maine: Hoyt, Fogg & Donham, 1875), p. 104. John Cotton's conversion experiences (p. 35) are described by Sister R. Mildred Barker in *Holy Land: A History of the Alfred Shakers* (Sabbathday Lake, Maine: The Shaker Press, 1983), p. 3. See also Usher Parsons, *A Centennial History of Alfred, York County, Maine* (Philadelphia: Sanford, Everts & Co., 1872). The sampling of Mother Ann's precepts (pp. 36-37) is quoted from the second edition of Bishop and Wells, *Testimonies*, pp. 208, 210, 211, 212, 242-43, as are the statements of her brother, William (quoted on p. 37), p. 265. Sister Mildred's *Holy Land*, pp. 6-8 is the source of the story (pp. 37-38) of the journey of the Maine Shakers to visit Mother Ann and their momentous return home. Her account relies heavily on Otis Sawyer, "Alfred, Me.," *The Manifesto* 15 (January, 1885, 11-12: February, 1885, 33-34; March, 1885, 58-59). Sister Aurelia G. Mace recorded her impressions in an untitled manuscript commonplace book preserved in the archives at Sabbathday Lake. The description of the meetinghouse (pp. 39-40) is her entry for September 18-19, 1896. The stories quoted on pp. 45-46 and 46-47 are also from this source, respectively the entries for March 23, 1896 and March 20, 1896. Elder Otis Sawyer's address at *The New Gloucester Centennial*,

177

pp. 100-109, outlines much of the early history of the community, the construction of its buildings and the establishment of its trades as referred to on pp. 38-40 and elsewhere in this chapter. Nineteenth-century Believers were excellent record keepers and the official journals of the Church are indispensable sources for the community's history. The excerpt quoted on p. 41 is from the manuscript, "Church Record. New Gloucester Vol. 4," p. 118, in the hand of Eldress Mary Ann Gillespie. Seth Youngs Wells, comp. *Millennial Praises* (Hancock, Massachusetts: Josiah Tallcott, Jr., 1813), p. iv, is the source of the quote on p. 44. The account of Granville Merrill's first confession is from Aurelia G. Mace, *The Aletheia: Spirit of Truth*, Second Edition (Farmington, Maine: The Knowlton & McLeary Co., 1907), pp. 122-23. The excerpt (pp. 46-47) is from Anna White and Leila S. Taylor, *Shakerism: Its Meaning and Message* (Columbus, Ohio: Fred. J. Heer, 1904), pp. 373-74.

WINTER

In a 1985 project sponsored by the National Trust for Historic Preservation, the Sabbathday Lake Shakers inaugurated an oral history of the community. Richard C. J. Henderson, appointed as a Yankee Intern under this program, recorded the recollections of former Shakers and employees of the Society, including those of 99-year-old Elizabeth Washburn, a Shaker for twenty-five years in the early part of the century. This oral history is the source of the quotes on pp. 52 and 71. Sister R. Mildred Barker's description of the sisters' winter companionship (p. 54) is from her "Home Notes from Sabbathday Lake, Maine," *The Shaker Quarterly* 6 (Spring, 1966), p. 21. A remarkable ten-record album produced by William Randle, *The Shaker Heritage* (Cleveland: Western Reserve University, 1960-1961) is the source of the quotation from Elder Delmer C. Wilson on p. 57. It may be heard among this faithful brother's other reminiscences on Side 17. The story of Mother Ann and Hannah Hocknell (p. 58) may be found in several Shaker sources. It is quoted here from Brother Theodore E. Johnson, "Concerning Our Yearly

Fast," *The Shaker Quarterly* 9 (Winter 1969, p. 141). Elder Otis Sawyer's record of Christmas, 1845 (p. 59) is transcribed by Brother Theodore E. Johnson in "Introduction to the Christmas Meeting of December 25th 1845 on Chosen Land," *The Shaker Quarterly* 7 (Winter 1967, pp. 126, 127, 131). This is also the source of the quote on p. 61; it appears on p. 121 of Brother Theodore's article. Sister Aurelia G. Mace's untitled manuscript commonplace book in the library at Sabbathday Lake contains a copy of her letter to the editors of the *Lewiston Journal* (quoted on p. 61) in her entry of February 9-11, 1896. The Christmas sentiment (p. 62) is from Sister R. Mildred Barker, "Simplicity: God's Christmas Gift to Man," *The Shaker Quarterly* 10 (Winter 1970, pp. 112-13). Sister Mildred's New Year's musings (p. 63) are from her "Home Notes from Sabbathday Lake, Maine," *The Shaker Quarterly* 7 (Spring 1967, p. 10). Daniel W. Patterson's notes in the booklet accompanying the Sabbathday Lake Shakers' recording, *Early Shaker Spirituals* (Somerville, Massachusetts: Rounder Records), p. 11, is the source of the story of the Shepherdess (p. 66). The song that this mysterious figure inspired may be heard on Side A, Band III of the record. The quotation on pp. 68-69 is from Lucy S. Bowers, *Concise Statements Concerning the Life and Religious Views of the Shakers* (Mount Lebanon, New York: North Family, ca. 1895), p. 6. The story of Shaker poplar ware is told by Sister Elsie A. McCool in her "Shaker Woven Poplar Ware," *The Shaker Quarterly* 2 (Summer 1962, pp. 56-59). This article is the source of the quotation on pp. 80-81. The song on p. 81 is entitled "Not One Sparrow;" it appears in *Shaker Music: Original Inspirational Hymns and Songs* on p. 97.

SPRING

"Springtime," the song appearing on p. 83, is from *Original Shaker Music Published by the North Family* (New York: Wm. A. Pond & Company, 1893), p. 102. The vision of Mother Ann extending her protection to animals (p. 84) is recorded in Anna White and Leila S. Taylor, *Shakerism: Its Meaning and Message* (Columbus, Ohio: Fred.

J. Heer, 1904), pp. 243-44. The story of Moses and Dmitri (p. 84) is from "The United Society of Shakers, Sabbathday Lake," *The Shaker Messenger* 7 (Fall 1984, p. 19). Sister Frances A. Carr's "Mother Lucy's Sayings Spoken at Different Times and under Various Circumstances," *The Shaker Quarterly* 8 (Winter 1968, p. 105), is the source of the quotations on pp. 88-89. New Gloucester pride about the importance of local lumbering (pp. 89-90) is quoted in T.H. Haskell, *The New Gloucester Centennial* (Portland, Me.: Hoyt, Fogg & Donham, 1875), p. 48. Brother Delmer's memories of tapping maple trees (p. 90) are recorded on Side 17 of William Randle's *The Shaker Heritage* (Cleveland: Western Reserve University, 1960-61). Sister Mildred's "Home Notes from Sabbathday Lake," *The Shaker Quarterly* 6 (Summer 1966, p. 48) is the source of her quote on p. 92. One of a series of almanacs advertising Shaker pharmaceutical products from Mount Lebanon, New York, *The 100th Anniversary of the Founding of a Community. Almanac for 1888* (New York: A.J. White, 1887) contains the material quoted on p. 98; the excerpt appears in the source on p. 27. Of the many important contributions of Brother Theodore E. Johnson to the pages of *The Shaker Quarterly* (which appeared under his editorship from 1961-1974), one of the most intriguing is "The Great 'Portland Meetings' of 1872," *The Shaker Quarterly* 12 (Winter 1972, pp. 121-37). It is the source of much of the material on public meetings referred to on p. 102 of this chapter. The acquisition of Elder Oliver's flax wheel (p. 103) is recounted by Sister Mildred in her "Home Notes from Sabbathday Lake, Maine," *The Shaker Quarterly* (Summer 1966). Aurelia G. Mace, *The Aletheia: Spirit of Truth*, Second Edition (Farmington, Maine: Knowlton & McLeary Co., 1907), pp. 33-36, is the source of the quotation on p. 104. Her letter is dated June 1883.

SUMMER

The song that opens this chapter (p. 111) is from *Shaker Music: Original Inspirational Hymns and Songs* (New York: William A. Pond & Co.,

1884), p. 218. Wendell May's recollections as one of Elder Delmer Wilson's hired men (pp. 112-13) are preserved in a recording made at Sabbathday Lake in 1985 by Richard C.J. Henderson in the oral history project sponsored by the National Trust for Historic Preservation. The story of another hired man, as told by Eldresses Hester Ann Adams and Mary Ann Gillespie (pp. 113-14), is recorded in a manuscript letter, dated May 7, 1877, from Eldresses Eliza Ann Taylor and Polly J. Reed to the eldresses of the Groveland, New York, church (New York Public Library, Manuscripts and Archives Division ms. 65M93). H.A. Poole and G.W. Poole, *History of Poland, Embracing a Period of Over a Century* (Mechanic Falls, Me.: Poole Publishers, 1890) pp. 28-29, is the source of the tale of the clock repairman and Elder Nehemiah Trull (p. 114). All accounts of early Shaker history rely heavily on Rufus Bishop and Seth Youngs Wells, eds., *Testimonies of the Life, Character, Revelations and Doctrines of Our Ever Blessed Mother Ann Lee, and the Elders with Her* (Hancock, Massachusetts: J. Tallcott & J. Deming, Jrs., 1816), an exceedingly rare and important work. It is the source of the account of Father James Whittaker's vision quoted in this chapter on p. 114. The excerpt may be found on p. 66 in the original work. It is also the source of the story of the Shakers' voyage to America (p. 122). "Rights of Conscience," the hymn appearing on p. 115 was first published, without music, in Seth Youngs Wells, comp., *Millennial Praises* (Hancock, Massachusetts: Josiah Tallcott, Jr., 1812-1813), pp. 281-85. There are fifteen stanzas in all; the quoted portion appears on pp. 281-82 in the source. Daniel W. Patterson provides words and music in *The Shaker Spiritual* (Princeton: Princeton University Press, 1979), pp. 165–67. John Holmes's defense of Shaker rights (p. 120) is quoted from *The Debate and Journals of the Constitutional Convention of the State of Maine 1819–'20* (Augusta: Maine Farmers' Almanac Press, 1894), p. 256, which incorporates Jeremiah Perley's original account of these proceedings, as published in 1820. Leila S. Taylor, *A Memorial To Eldress Anna White and Elder Daniel Offord* (Mount Lebanon, New York: North Family of Shakers,

1912), p. 77, is the source of Eldress Anna's plea for peace quoted on p. 121. One of the most moving and delightful sources for the history of twentieth-century Shakerism in Maine is contained on Side 19 of William Randle's *The Shaker Heritage* in the recorded memories of Sister R. Mildred Barker. Sister Mildred's reminiscences of her first experiences among Believers at Alfred (pp. 121-22) and of learning Shaker traditions in music and dance from the older sisters (p. 127) are transcribed from this recording. Sister Aurelia G. Mace's commonplace book is the source for the story of Elder Oliver Holmes' anthem (p. 125), where it appears as the entry for March 27, 1896, as well as for the description of the Shaker "march" or dance in worship (p. 126), entry for April 6-7, 1896. The excerpt from the *Lewiston Journal* (p. 129) is quoted from "A Sunday with the Shakers," *Shaker Manifesto* 11 (October 1881), p. 226. Sister Aurelia's letter (p. 129) may be found in her *The Aletheia: Spirit of Truth*, Second Edition (Farmington, Maine: The Knowlton & McLeary Co., 1907), pp. 66-67. Her comments on the Shaker cap (p. 131) is from the "Church Record, New Gloucester, Volume 4," entry for March 26, 1896, as is her comments on the attempts of the brethren to ride a bicycle (p. 142), entry for July 27, 1896. Theodore E. Johnson's observations about primitive Maine Shaker furniture (p. 133) are from his *In the Eye of Eternity: Shaker Life and the Work of Shaker Hands* (Gorham, Maine: The United Society of Shakers and the University of Southern Maine, 1983), p. 10. The story of Sister Aurelia and Charles Tiffany (p. 137) is told in Joseph Purtell, *The Tiffany Touch* (New York: Random House, 1971), p. 111, the source of the quoted material here. Purtell relies on an unidentified newspaper report, reproduced as an illustration in his book.

FALL

"Autumn Song" (p. 145) may be found on p. 246 of *Shaker Music: Original Inspirational Hymns and Songs* (New York: William A. Pond & Co., 1894). The source of Mother Lucy Wright's sayings (pp. 148 and 153-54) is "Remarks of Mother Lucy Wright," *The Manifesto* 26 (July 1896, p. 113, and November 1896, p. 170). The story of Granville Merrill and tobacco (p. 149) may be found in Aurelia G. Mace, *The Aletheia: Spirit of Truth*, Second Edition (Farmington, Maine: The Knowlton & McLeary Co., 1907), p. 126. Anna White and Leila S. Taylor, *Shakerism: Its Meaning and Message* (Columbus, Ohio: Fred J. Heer, 1904), pp. 161-62, is the source of the Nancy Lockwood story (p. 149). The visit to the children's order (pp. 150-51) is recorded by Jean May Thompson in "Passing the Shaker," *Harper's Bazaar*, 44 (June 1910, p. 376). The material quoted about the Douglas family (p. 152) is from the manuscript "Church Record, Gloucester, Vol. 3," p. 121, in the hand of Eldress Mary Ann Gillespie. Sister Aurelia G. Mace's manuscript commonplace book is the source of the story of young Israel Cushman (p. 152), where it appears as the entry for March 28-29, 1896. This work is also the source of the story about Otis Sawyer (p. 153), entry for April 10, 1896. The second edition of Sister Aurelia's *Aletheia*, p. 9, records her musings about the "Celestial March" (p. 152, as well as her statement on God the Mother (p. 156), which appears on pp. 140-41 of the original. The quotation of the unidentified sister (p. 154) is from C. Talbot Rogers, "The People called Shakers," *Down East 4* (October 1957, p. 21). Sister R. Mildred Barker's Thanksgiving thoughts (p. 167) are from her "Home Notes from Sabbathday Lake, Maine," *The Shaker Quarterly* 10 (Winter 1970, p. 120). "All Things Anew" (p. 170) is an excerpt from an eloquent statement of rededication by the Sabbathday Lake Shakers appearing in *The Shaker Quarterly* 12 (Winter 1972, pp. 119, 120).

Bibliography

Adam, David. "Shaker Herbs: Revitalizing a Century-Old Industry." *The Maine Organic Farmer & Gardener* 3 (November-December 1976): 1.

"A Sunday with the Shakers." *The Shaker Manifesto* 11 (October 1881): 225–27.

Andrews, Edward Deming. *The People Called Shakers: A Search for the Perfect Society.* New York: Oxford University Press, 1953.

Barker, R. Mildred. "A History of 'Holy Land'— Alfred, Maine." *The Shaker Quarterly* 3 (Fall 1963): 75–95; (Winter 1963): 107–27. (Reissued in 1983 by The Shaker Press, Sabbathday Lake, Maine, as a pamphlet under the title *Holy Land: A History of the Alfred Shakers.*)

———. "A Shaker Viewpoint on the Authority of the Bible." *The Shaker Quarterly* 1 (Winter 1961): 140–44.

———. "Eldress Harriett N. Coolbroth's 'I Will Walk More Closely with Thee.'" *The Shaker Quarterly* 10 (Spring 1970): 3–7.

———. "History of Union Branch, Gorham, Maine, 1784–1819." *The Shaker Quarterly* 7 (Summer 1967): 64–82.

———. "Home Notes from Sabbathday Lake, Maine." *The Shaker Quarterly* 1–14 (1961–1974).

———. "In Memoriam. Eva May Libby. 1872–1966." *The Shaker Quarterly* 6 (Spring 1966): 3–4.

———. "Mother Has Come with Her Beautiful Song." *The Shaker Quarterly* 4 (Winter 1964): 128–29.

———. "Our Mother in the New Creation." *The Shaker Quarterly* 1 (Spring 1961): 10–15.

———. "Revelation: A Shaker Viewpoint." *The Shaker Quarterly* 3 (Spring 1963): 7–17.

———. "Simplicity: God's Christmas Gift to Man." *The Shaker Quarterly* 10 (Winter 1970): 107–15.

———. *The Sabbathday Lake Shakers: An Introduction to the Shaker Heritage.* Sabbathday Lake, Maine: The Shaker Press, 1978.

Belanger, Gretchen. "Herbalist Brings Growth to Sabbathday Lake Shaker Community." *Countryside* 61 (January 1977): 26–28.

[Bishop, Rufus, and Seth Youngs Wells, eds.] *Testimonies of the Life, Character, Revelations and Doctrines of Mother Ann Lee, and the Elders with Her, Through Whom the Word of Eternal Life Was Opened in This Day, of Christ's Second Appearing, Collected from Living Witnesses, in Union with the Church.* Second edition, [Giles B. Avery, ed.] Albany, New York: Weed, Parsons & Co., 1888.

———. *Testimonies of the Life, Character, Revelations and Doctrines of Our Ever Blessed Mother Ann Lee, and the Elders with Her: Through Whom the Word of Eternal Life Was Opened in This Day of Christ's Second Appearing: Collected from Living Witnesses, by Order of the Ministry, in Union with the Church.* Hancock, Massachusetts: J. Tallcott & J. Deming, Junrs., 1816.

[Blinn, Henry C., comp.] *A Sacred Repository of Anthems and Hymns, for Devotional Worship and Praise.* Canterbury, New Hampshire: [Shaker Society], 1852.

Blinn, Henry C. *The Manifestation of Spiritualism among the Shakers, 1837–1847.* East Canterbury, New Hampshire: [Shaker Society], 1899.

Bourgeault, Cynthia. "Hands to Work, Hearts to God." *Down East* 31 (December 1984): 34–39, 62–63.

Bowdoin College Museum of Art. *Hands to Work and Hearts to God: the Shaker Tradition in Maine.* [Exhibition catalogue]. Essay and notes by Theodore E. Johnson; photographs by John McKee. Brunswick, Maine: Bowdoin College Museum of Art, 1969.

[Bowers, Lucy S.] *Concise Statements Concerning the Life and Religious Views of the Shakers.* Mount Lebanon, N.Y.: North Family [ca. 1895].

Carpenter, Mary Grace, and Charles H. Carpenter, Jr. "The Shaker Furniture of Elder Henry Green." *Antiques* 105 (May 1974): 1119–25.

Carr, Frances A. "A Letter to Jennifer, written from Chosen Land, August 6, 1974." *The Shaker Quarterly* 14 (Fall 1974): 84–86.

———. "Mother Lucy's Sayings Spoken at Different Times and Under Various Circumstances." *The Shaker Quarterly* 8 (March 1968): 99–106.

———. "The New Gloucester Shaker School and Its Teachers." *The Shaker Quarterly* 1 (Spring 1961): 16–20.

———. *Shaker Your Plate: Of Shaker Cooks and Cooking.* Sabbathday Lake, Maine: United Society of Shakers, 1985.

———. "The Shakers as Herb Growers." *The Shaker Quarterly* 3 (Summer 1963): 39–43.

———. "The Tamar Fruit Compound: A Maine Shaker Industry." *The Shaker Quarterly* 2 (Spring 1962): 39–41.

Catalog of Fancy Goods Made at Shaker Village, Alfred,

York County, Maine. Fannie C. Casey, Trustee and General Manager, 1908. Reissued as a facsimile reprint by Sabbathday Lake Shakers in 1971 as "Hands to Work Series No. 1."

Catalogue of Herbs, Roots, Barks, Powdered Articles, &c., Prepared in the United Society, New Gloucester, Maine. Portland, Maine: B. Thurston, 1864. Reissued as a facsimile reprint by Sabbathday Lake Shakers in 1972 as "Hands to Work Series No. 2."

"Chosen Land: A Photographic Essay." *The Shaker Quarterly* 1 (Summer 1961): 62–70.

"Christmas Hymn—1807." *The Shaker Quarterly* 4 (Winter 1964): 118–22.

"Church Record." Vols. 1–5. Manuscript journals in the Library of the United Society of Shakers, Sabbathday Lake, Maine.

[Clayton, W. Woodford, comp.] *History of Cumberland Co., Maine. With Illustrations and Biographical Sketches.* Philadelphia: Everts & Peck, 1880.

———. *History of York Co., Maine. With Illustrations and Biographical Sketches.* Philadelphia: Everts & Peck, 1880.

Coolbroth, Gennie M. *A Concise Answer to the Many Questions Asked by the Public.* Sabbathday Lake, Maine: [Shaker Society], 1933.

[Cummings, Ada S., comp.] *In Memoriam: Sister Aurelia G. Mace. 1835–1910.* Portland, Maine: George Loring, 1910.

———. "Notes about Home—Sabbathday Lake, Me." *The Manifesto* 21–29 (1891–1899).

The Debates and Journals of the Constitutional Convention of the State of Maine 1819–20. Augusta: Maine Farmers' Almanac Press, 1894. Incorporates Jeremiah Perley, *The Debates, Resolutions and Other Proceedings of the Convention of Delegates,* originally published 1820 in Portland by A. Shirley.

Filley, Dorothy M. *Recapturing Wisdom's Valley: The Watervliet Shaker Heritage, 1775–1975.* Albany, New York: The Town of Colonie and the Albany Institute of History and Art, 1975.

[Green, Calvin, and Seth Youngs Wells.] *A Summary View of the Millennial Church, or United Society of Believers, (Commonly Called Shakers.) Comprising the Rise, Progress and Practical Order of the Society; together with the General Principles of Their Faith and Testimony.* Albany, New York: Packard & Van Benthuysen, 1823.

Haskell, Della. "What is Shakerism?" *The Shaker Quarterly* 1 (Spring 1961): 21–25.

Haskell, T. H., ed. *The New Gloucester Centennial, September 7, 1874.* Portland, Maine: Hoyt, Fogg & Donham, 1875.

Hutchinson, Gloria. "The Shakers of Sabbathday Lake." *Down East* 18 (October 1971) 38–41, 66–67, 70, 75, 77.

"In Memoriam. Delmer Charles Wilson. 1873–1961." *The Shaker Quarterly* 1 (Winter 1961): 135–36.

Johnson, Theodore E., ed. "Elder Otis Sawyer's 'A Complete Register of All the Deaths that Have Occurred in the United Societies of Gorham and New Gloucester, Maine.'" *The Shaker Quarterly* 1 (Spring 1961): 32–42.

———. "Eldress Mary Ann Gillespie's 'Beautiful Are They Who Stand upon Mt. Zion.'" *The Shaker Quarterly* 10 (Winter 1970): 141–44.

———. *In the Eye of Eternity: Shaker Life and the Work of Shaker Hands.* Gorham, Maine: The United Society of Shakers and the University of Southern Maine, 1983.

———. "Ingenious and Useful: Shaker Sisters' Communal Industries, 1860–1940." Exhibition checklist. Sabbathday Lake, Maine: United Society of Shakers, 1985.

———. "Introduction to the Christmas Meeting of Dec. 25th 1845 on Chosen Land." *The Shaker Quarterly* 7 (Winter 1967): 119–31.

———. "Life in the Christ Spirit: Observations on Shaker Theology." *The Shaker Quarterly* 8 (Fall 1968): 67–76. Also issued by the Sabbathday Lake Shakers as a separate pamphlet.

———. "The Diary of a Maine Shaker Boy: Delmer Wilson—1887." *The Shaker Quarterly* 8 (Spring 1968): 3–22.

———. "The Great 'Portland Meetings' of 1872." *The Shaker Quarterly* 12 (Winter 1972): 121–37.

Mace, Aurelia G. *The Aletheia: Spirit of Truth.* Second Edition. Farmington, Maine: Press of The Knowlton & McLeary Co., 1907.

———. Untitled manuscript commonplace book, 1896–1908, in the Library of the United Society of Shakers, Sabbathday Lake, Maine.

Manchester, England. *The Constables' Accounts for the Manor of Manchester.* Ed. by J. P. Earwaker. Manchester: H. Blacklock and Co., 1892.

Marini, Stephen A. *Radical Sects of Revolutionary New England.* Cambridge, Massachusetts: Harvard University Press, 1982.

Martin, Lucy. "Reviving the Shaker Herb Industry." *Maine Times* 9 (September 9, 1977): 16–17.

McCool, Elsie A. "A Brief History of the Central Dwelling, Sabbathday Lake." *The Shaker Quarterly* 1 (Summer 1961): 71–76.

———. "A Brief History of the Shaker Mills." *The Shaker Quarterly* 3 (Fall 1963): 99–102.

———, comp. "Gleanings from Sabbathday Lake Church Journals, 1872–1884." With an introduction by Theodore E. Johnson. *The Shaker Quarterly* 6 (Fall 1966): 103–12; (Winter 1966): 124–34.

———. "Shaker Woven Poplar Work." *The Shaker Quarterly* 2 (Summer 1962): 55–59.

[Meacham, Joseph.] *A Concise Statement of the Principles of the Only True Chruch According to the Gospel of the Present Appearance of Christ.* Bennington, Vermont: Haswell & Russell, 1790. Reprinted in 1963 by the Sabbathday Lake Shakers as "Mother's Work Series No. 2."

Merrill, Georgia Drew, ed. *History of Androscoggin County, Maine.* Boston, Massachusetts: W. A. Ferguson & Co., 1891.

National Heritage Fellowships: 1983. Washington, D.C.: National Endowment for the Arts and The Smithsonian Institution: 1983.

[Offord, Daniel, and others, comps.] *Original Shaker Music Published by the North Family. Of Mt. Lebanon, Columbia Co., N.Y.* New York: Wm. A. Pond & Company, 1893.

———. *Shaker Music: Original Inspirational Hymns and Songs Illustrative of the Resuurection of Life and Testimony of the Shakers.* New York: William A. Pond & Co. for the North Family, Mount Lebanon, N.Y., 1884.

Parsons, Usher. *A Centennial History of Alfred, York County, Maine.* Philadelphia, Pennsylvania: Sanford, Everts & Co., 1872.

Patterson, Daniel W. *Early Shaker Spirituals.* Notes accompanying recording of Shaker music sung by Sisters R. Mildred Barker, Ethel Peacock, Elsie McCool, Della Haskell, Frances Carr and other members of the United Society of Shakers, Sabbathday Lake, Maine. Somerville, Massachusetts: Rounder Records, 1976.

———. *Gift Drawing and Gift Song: A Study of Two Forms of Shaker Inspiration.* Sabbathday Lake, Maine: The United Society of Shakers, 1983.

———. *The Shaker Spiritual.* Princeton, New Jersey: Princeton University Press, 1979.

Péladeau, Marius B. "Anyone for St. Johnswort?" *Down East* 20 (July 1974): 64–67.

———. "The Shaker Meetinghouses of Moses Johnson." *Antiques* 98 (October 1970): 594–99.

Philbrook, Eleanor. "A Brief History of the Shaker Post Office. Sabbathday Lake, Maine." *The Shaker Quarterly* 4 (Spring 1964): 38–40.

Piercy, Caroline B. *The Shaker Cook Book: Not by Bread Alone.* New York: Crown Publishing, Inc., 1953.

Poole, H. A., and G. W. Poole. *History of Poland: Embracing a Period of Over a Century.* Mechanic Falls, Maine: Poole Publishers, 1890.

Purtell, Joseph. *The Tiffany Touch.* New York: Random House, Inc., 1971.

"Remarks of Mother Lucy Wright." *The Manifesto* 26 (April 1896): 65–66; (July 1896): 113–14; (November 1896): 169–70.

Robinson, Charles Edson. *A Concise History of the United Society of Believers called Shakers.* East Canterbury, New Hampshire: [Shaker Society], 1893.

Rogers, C. Talbot. "The People Called Shakers." *Down East* 4 October 1957): 20–23.

Sabbathday Lake Shakers. "All Things Anew." *The Shaker Quarterly* 12 (Winter 1972): 119–20.

———. "The United Society of Shakers, Sabbathday Lake." *The Shaker Messenger* 7 (Fall, 1984): 19.

Sawyer, Otis. "Alfred, Me." *The Manifesto* 15 (January 1885): 11–12; (February 1885): 33–34; (March 1885): 58–59.

———. "Concerning Our Yearly Fast." Ed. with an introduction by Theodore E. Johnson. *The Shaker Quarterly* 9 (Winter 1969): 141–47.

Schwartz, Hillel. *The French Prophets: The History of a Millennarian Group in Eighteenth-Century England.* Berkeley, California: University of California Press, 1980.

Shaker Church Covenant. East Canterbury, New Hampshire: [Shaker Society], 1906.

Sommer, Margaret Van Alen Frisbee. *The Shaker Garden Seed Industry.* Orono, Maine: University of Maine, 1966.

Stewart, I. D. *The History of the Freewill Baptists, for Half a Century, with an Introductory Chapter.* Dover, New Hampshire: Freewill Baptist Printing Establishment, 1862.

Taylor, Leila S. *A Memorial to Eldress Anna White, and Elder Daniel Offord.* Mount Lebanon, New York: North Family of Shakers, 1912.

The 100th. Anniversary of the Founding of a Community. Almanac for 1888. New York: A. J. White, 1887.

Thompson, Jean May. "Passing of the Shaker." *Harper's Bazar* 44 (June 1910): 376–77.

[Wells, Seth Youngs, comp.] *Millennial Praises; Containing a Collection of Gospel Hymns, in Four Parts, Adapted to the Day of Christ's Second Appearing.* Hancock, Massachusetts: Josiah Tallcott, Junior, 1813.

Wertkin, Gerard C. " 'The Flame Is Never Ceasing': Continuity in Shaker Life at Sabbathday Lake." *The Clarion* (Fall 1979): 58–67.

Whitcher, Mary. *Mary Whitcher's Shaker House-Keeper.* Boston: Weeks & Potter, c. 1882.

White, Anna, and Leila S. Taylor. *Shakerism: Its Meaning and Message.* Columbus, Ohio: Press of Fred. J. Heer, 1904.

Whitney, Stephen T. "Shaker Baked Goodies." *Yankee* (November 1970): 168–70.

Index

Meacham, Joseph, 32, 38, 44, 45, 57, 68, 91, 118, 126, 155, 156
meetinghouses, 38–40
Merrill, Edmund, 34
Merrill, Granville, 46, 81, 90, 113, 149
Merrill, James, Sr., 37
Merrill, Mary, 34, 35
Merrill family, 34
"Merry Dancers," 32, 35
metric measures, 81, 90
millenarian religions, 24
Millennial Praises, 44, 118, 124
Millerites, 47
Ministry's Shop, 39, 91, 102
Mint Vinegar Dressing, 139
"Mother," 123, 124
Mother Ann, *see* Lee, Ann
Mother Ann's Cake, 66
Mother Ann's Day, 66
"Mother Has Come With Her Beautiful Song," 128, 129
"Mother Lucy's Sayings," 88–89
Mother Seigel's Curative Syrup, 98
Mount Lebanon, N.Y., 46–47, 55, 69, 81, 88, 96, 98, 105, 120, 121, 129, 139
mourning customs, 165–67
Muggletonians, 24
music, *see* songs

Neale, Emma, 47
New Gloucester, Maine, 17, 32, 40, 46, 89, 96, 98, 102, 118–20, 126, 136, 137, 153, 156
"New Gloucester Church Journal," 41, 57, 142
New Lebanon, N.Y., 32, 35, 38, 47, 80, 92, 137, 149, 153, 157
"New Light" revival, 32, 35, 47
"New Lights," 32
New Year holiday, 62–63
"New Year's Greeting," 63
New York Times, 120
Niskayuna, N.Y., 27, 32, 37, 58
nonconformists, 24
North Union, Ohio, 38
Norwood's Tincture of Veratrum Viride, 98
"Notes about Home" (Cummings), 52, 143, 152
Nowell, Betty, 103
Nowell, Paul, 149
Noyes, Elizabeth M., 17, 19, 69, 90, 142
Noyes, Josiah, 105
Noyes, Thomas, 149
Nutter, Ruth Perkins, 112, 136
Nutter & Kimball, 137

oak shooks, 81, 90, 91, 137
Old Chatham, N.Y., the Shaker Museum at, 136
orchards, 80, 92, 146
Order of Zion, 91
Original Shaker Music, 83

Palmer, Sarah, 153
Parker, David, 157
Partington, John, 25, 27
Partington, Mary, 122
patent medicines, 96–101
Patterson, Daniel W., 124, 156
Paul, William, 149
Peacock, Ethel, 101, 102, 103, 146
Pelham, Joseph, 55
People's News, 129
Edward D. Pettengill Co., 150
pharmaceutical herb business, 92–102
Philbrook, Eleanor, 112, 136

Philpot, Margaret, 120
Pierce, Eddie, 90
Pierce, Franklin, 120
Pleasant Hill, Ky., 38, 105
Poland Hill, Maine, 40, 46, 57, 89, 102, 113–14, 153
Poland Spring House, 137, 139, 142, 150, 156
Pote, Dorothy, 34, 35
Pote, Elisha, 32, 34, 35, 133–34
Pote family, 34
Prescott, Lucy, 38, 153

Quakers (Society of Friends), 24, 27, 120

Randall, Benjamin, 32, 34, 35
Ranters, 24
Rebecca of Sunnybrook Farm (Wiggin), 54
recipes:
    The Brethren's Cider, 149
    Candied Sweet Flag, 101
    Mint Vinegar Dressing, 139
    Shaker Applesauce, 146
    Sister Frances' Turkey with Bread Stuffing, 168
    Sister Minnie's White Bread, 76
    Strawberry Summer Pudding, 142
    Stringbean and Mushroom Salad, 139
    Traditional Holiday Boiled Fruit Cake, 61
"Redeeming Love," 8, 9
Reed, Matilda, 46–47
Reed, Polly Jane, 55, 69
"Resurrection," 88–89
Resurrection Life, 88
revival movements, 32–34, 35, 47
Ricker, E. P., 104
Ricker family, 139
"Rights of Conscience," 115
Ring family, 34
Roosevelt, Theodore, 121
Royal River (Maine), 17
rug weaving, 105

Sabbathday Lake community:
    baking at, 71
    canning and preserving at, 150
    Christmas celebrations at, 59, 61–62
    construction at, 38–39, 40
    description of, 8, 16–17
    establishment of, 34
    "expanded" summer family at, 112–15, 142–43
    fall activities at, 145–69
    floriculture at, 142
    Fourth of July celebration at, 114
    Friends of the Shakers' gathering at, 131
    Great Mill at, 80, 89–90, 104, 105, 112, 161
    harvest activities at, 146
    herb business at, 92–102
    industries at, 80–81, 89–90, 92–102, 104–9
    Institute for Shaker Studies at, 155
    livestock at, 84–86
    maple syrup production at, 90–91
    mealtime customs at, 71–76
    meetinghouse at, 39–40
    naming of, 16
    New Year celebration at, 62–63
    planting season at, 91–92, 101
    public meetings at, 102
    publishing activities at, 155–56
    schoolhouse at, 153–54
    seed business at, 92–96